GCSE **CDT-TECHNOLOGY**

GUIDES

LONGMAN REVISE GUIDES

SERIES EDITORS
Geoff Black and Stuart Wall

TITLES AVAILABLE
Art and Design
Biology
Business Studies
CDT - Design and Realisation
CDT - Technology
Chemistry
Computer Studies
Economics
English*
English Literature*
French
Geography
German
Home Economics
Mathematics*
Mathematics: Higher Level and Extension
Music
Physics
Religious Studies
Science*
World History

* New editions for Key Stage 4

LONGMAN

REVISE

GUIDES

GCSE
CDT-TECHNOLOGY

Keith Simmonds

Longman

Longman Group UK Limited,
Longman House, Burnt Mill, Harlow,
Essex CM20 2JE, England
and Associated Companies throughout the world.

© Longman Group Limited 1990

First published 1990
Third Impression 1993

British Library Cataloguing in Publication Data

Simmonds, Keith
 CDT – technology.
 1. England. Secondary Schools. Curriculum subjects:
 Design G.C.S.E. examinations.
 I. Title
 745.4'076

 ISBN 0–582–02507–9

Set in 10/12pt Century Old Style

Produced by Longman Singapore Publishers Pte Ltd
Printed in Singapore

CONTENTS

EDITORS' PREFACE

Longman Revise Guides are written by experienced examiners and teachers, and aim to give you the best possible foundation for success in examinations and other modes of assessment. Examiners are well aware that the performance of many candidates falls short of their true potential, and this series of books aims to remedy this by encouraging thorough study and a full understanding of the concepts involved. The Revise Guides should be seen as course companions and study aids to be used throughout the year, not just for last-minute revision.

Examiners are in no doubt that a structured approach in preparing for examinations and in presenting coursework can, together with hard work and diligent application, substantially improve performance.

The largely self-contained nature of each chapter gives the book a useful degree of flexibility. After starting with the opening general chapters on the background to the GCSE and syllabus coverage, all other chapters can be read selectively, in any order appropriate to the stage you have reached in your course.

We believe that this book, and the series as a whole, will help you establish a solid platform of basic knowledge and examination technique on which to build.

Geoff Black and Stuart Wall

ACKNOWLEDGEMENTS

Grateful acknowledgement is made for the assistance given by the following: Mr L.A. Sampson, University of London Examinations and Assessment Council (which accepts no responsibility whatsoever for the accuracy or method of working in the answers given); Midland Examining Group; Southern Examining Group; Northern Examinations and Assessment Board; Welsh Joint Education Committee. I am grateful to these bodies for permission to quote from their syllabuses and question papers.

My grateful thanks to Mr A. Lyons for his support, and to my wife and family for their support and considerable patience.

I would like to dedicate this book to the many teaching and examining colleagues I have met and worked with, and to the many students I have taught and candidates whose work I have seen; they have provided me with the experience which made this task possible.

GCSE IN CDT: TECHNOLOGY

ALLOCATION OF MARKS

TYPES OF SYLLABUS

ASSESSMENT

PURPOSE OF TECHNOLOGY

ADDRESSES OF THE EXAM GROUPS

GETTING STARTED

Craft, Design and Technology (CDT) is a course title that includes three separate courses:

1 Technology.
2 Design and Realisation.
3 Design and Communication.

The three courses have many aspects of work in common with each other. So if you are doing more than one of the courses you will not have to learn three completely different areas of knowledge and skills.

This book is going to look in detail at the courses in **Technology**. There are six Regional Examination Groups. Each offers a course approved under the CDT criteria in CDT: Technology; one group has a course approved under the Science criteria in Technology. Unless your school is using a special Mode 3 GCSE syllabus it is likely that you will be following one of these courses.

Several factors may influence the course you take.

a) **Where you live.** England, Wales and Northern Ireland have been split into six examination areas. In these areas a Regional Examinations Group has been set up to deal with all GCSE subjects. It is likely that you will take the course offered by your local Examinations Group.

b) **The school or college you attend.** Each school or college can choose the examination which it feels will best serve the needs of its pupils. This may mean that a school or college chooses a syllabus from an Examination group outside its own area.

c) **The Local Education Authority.** This is a team of people who are responsible for making sure that you have buildings, equipment and teachers. They are also concerned with your education and they are interested in seeing that their schools are providing you with the best possible chances within what they can afford to pay.

Usually your teachers will advise you which syllabus you will be taking. You can contact your own examination group to get your personal copy of the syllabus. The names and addresses of the examination groups are listed on page 6 so that you can write and request an order form. You will then have to complete the order form and enclose the cost of the syllabus and postage.

ESSENTIAL PRINCIPLES

To be examined at GCSE every syllabus must be submitted to, and approved by, the Secondary Examinations and Assessment Council (SEAC). This means that within certain limits all of the Technology syllabuses are very similar. So no matter where you live, or in which school or college you are being taught, you will be following a course that is similar to one in any part of the country.

1 > ALLOCATION OF MARKS

Table 1.1 shows how the **marks** for each course are divided.

GROUP	COURSEWORK	WRITTEN EXAM		DESIGN EXAM
	(PROJECT)	CORE	MODULES	
ULEAC	50%	10%	20%	20%
MEG	50%	10%	20%	20%
		Paper 1	Paper 2	
NEAB	50%	25%	25%	—
NISEAC	Grade C–G 45%	30%	25%	—
	Grade A–C 45%	20%	35%*	—
SEG	50%	20%	30%	—
WJEC	50%	20%	30%	—
	Mini project 20%			
	Major project 30%			

Table 1.1 Breakdown of course marks

* 15% Paper 2; 20% Paper 3.

2 > TYPES OF SYLLABUS

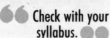

❝ Check with your syllabus. ❞

There are two main differences between the various syllabuses.

1   Some groups have combined the Design aspect of the examination with the coursework project, whilst others have a separate Design Paper which has to be done under examination conditions.
2   With the exception of the NEAB (syllabus A) all of the examinations have a modular structure for the *Written Papers*. This means that you have to sit a *Core Paper* plus two Optional Modules under examination conditions.

Table 1.2 shows the range of modules offered by each examination group.

MODULES	EXAM GROUP				
	ULEAC	MEG	SEG	WJEC	NISEAC
Materials		✓	✓		✓
Electronics	✓	✓	✓	✓	✓
Digital Microelectronics	✓		✓		
Digital Microelectronics and computer control	✓				
Structures			✓	✓	✓
Pneumatics	✓	✓		✓	
Mechanisms	✓	✓	✓	✓	✓
Instrumentation		✓			
Structures and Materials	✓				
Micro Processor Control				✓	

MODULES		EXAM GROUP				
		ULEAC	MEG	SEG	WJEC	NISEAC
Electronic Instrumentation					✓	
Bio Technology					✓	
Aeronautics			✓			
DOUBLE MODULES						
Control				✓		
Micro Processor Control				✓		
Number of modules to be taken		2	2	2 Single or 1 Double	3	2
Restrictions on choice			None		None	None

i) LEAG and SEG will not allow Electronics and Digital Microelectronics to be taken together.

ii) AERONAUTICS – subject to availability. Your teacher will tell you if this is available for your course.

iii) NISEC also have modules in Computing and Control, Electronic Systems and Fluid Power.

Table 1.2 Breakdown of courses with modular structure

Usually your teacher will tell you which of the optional modules you are studying. The choice made by your school or college will depend upon the type of equipment and rooms available and the number of Technology groups being taught.

Because of the differences between the modules offered by each examination group, it is important that you find out which course and modules you will be studying *before* you start the course.

All of the courses are intended to be completed in five terms, leaving the sixth term free for your final revision and the examinations. This means that you must follow the Technology course for the fourth and fifth year of school. However, you will have a better chance of success if you have followed some type of foundation course in CDT from the age of eleven.

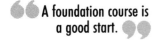 **A foundation course is a good start.**

3 > ASSESSMENT

Table 1.3 shows how your time is divided between the different parts of the examination.

GROUP	WRITTEN EXAM		DESIGN EXAM		COURSEWORK
	CORE	MODULES	PRE EXAM	EXAM	PROJECT(S)
ULEAC	2¼ hrs including core and 2 modules		A pr-exam (approx 1 month)	2 hrs	Final two terms Sept–May (approx 45 hrs)
MEG	40 mins core	1 hr 20 mins 2 modules	Themes 14 days before exam	2½ hrs	Final two terms Sept–May (approx 40 hrs)
NEAB	Paper 1 1½ hrs Not a core and module structure	Paper 2 1½ hrs	—	—	Final two terms Sept–April (approx 45 hrs)
NISEAC	Paper 1 1½ hrs	Papers 2/3 1 hr/1 hr	—	—	Final two terms Sept–April
SEG	Paper 1 1hr 30 mins core	Paper 2 2 hrs 2 modules or 1 double module	—	—	Final two terms Sept–May (Approx 45 hrs)
WJEC	Paper 1 1hr 30 mins core	Paper 2 3 hrs 3 modules	—	—	Two mini projects – from work in modules at any time during course Major project completion by 1 May

Table 1.3 Breakdown of time available for assessment

WRITTEN EXAMINATION

This consists of two parts

1   Core paper
2   Optional modules

There is very little difference between the Examination Groups in the *Core Paper*, however, the *Optional Modules* will reflect the titles offered by the different Examination Groups. Modules with the same title will cover similar areas of knowledge in all the Exam Groups.

Two slightly different styles of examination are used for the *Core Paper* and *Optional Modules*.

Style 1

Some groups have a paper where you are asked to attempt all the questions.

Style 2

Other groups have a paper where you have a section A with a series of shorter questions and a section B with two longer questions, from which you choose one.

Some Examinations use STYLE 1 for the *Core* and STYLE 2 for the *Optional Modules*.

All of the papers are designed by the Chief Examiners to help you to present your knowledge and thinking as clearly as possible. You will have a booklet with questions, diagrams, photographs and clearly marked spaces for your answers. Some exam groups use a 'theme' throughout the paper to help you further. You must be prepared to write, to do simple calculations and to draw diagrams as part of your answers.

Whilst many of the things you will be asked to do in the written examination are also assessed elsewhere in the course, you must be prepared to clearly show what you know **under examination conditions**. Your papers will then be sent away, to be marked by an examiner who does not know you as well as your teachers. It is important, therefore, that your answers clearly show your thinking and knowledge.

DESIGN EXAMINATION

ULEAC and MEG use a Design Paper as part of the technology examination structure. Both groups provide a pre-examination set of *themes* (MEG) and *questions* (ULEAC), approximately a month before you sit the Design Paper. During this time you can carry out *research* into your chosen theme or question. In the formal Design examination you will be given *specific* and *detailed questions* which relate to the pre-examination themes or questions.

For the MEG examination you are **not** allowed to take your research work from the pre-examination into the examination room. In the ULEAC examination you **are** allowed to take your research work into the examination room to use as reference material, but you must not do any further work on it.

In the Design examination you will be required to show your ability at *solving set problems* and *communicating your ideas* clearly. You will work on A3 drawing paper; some examination groups use pre-printed paper to help you.

Again your answer papers will be sent away to an examiner to be marked.

The other examination groups do not have a formal design examination. They look at your design abilities through the *design folder* or *folio* which forms part of your final project (coursework).

COURSEWORK

This is where the largest proportion of the marks are allocated. You should therefore spend the largest part of your time on this aspect of the course. In CDT: Technology, examination coursework usually takes the form of a 'terminal project'. This means that *you* undertake the *designing, making, testing* and *evaluating* of a major project during the last three terms of your course.

Some examination groups allow you to submit two smaller projects instead of one major project. The WJEC is rather different and requires you to do *two mini projects* as part of your work in the optional modules (10% of coursework marks for each project) and *one major project* (30% of coursework marks).

Find out if you have a choice.

'Positive' testing.

Know which applies to you.

Most marks are gained here.

Exactly what you do must be negotiated with your teacher and must meet the requirements of your examination group. If you wish you can work in groups, but it is important that **each member** of the group meets the requirements of the examination. Your coursework will be assessed by your teacher and moderated (checked) by an external examiner.

Whilst you can research your project and seek help from a variety of sources, it is important that the work is your **own**. Before you submit your project you will be asked to sign a declaration form, stating that it **is** your own work.

From the start of your course it is important that you know what is required. Sometimes it is useful to have a copy of the syllabus you are taking (see section 'Getting Started' at the beginning of this chapter). Ask your teacher if you can look at past examination papers to see how the questions are phrased and what the spaces for your answers are like. Remember, the more informed you are about the examination, the better you are likely to do.

4 ▷ PURPOSE OF TECHNOLOGY

Technology is principally concerned with the *design* and *problem-solving* processes, leading to the *making* and *evaluation* of artefacts and systems. It is concerned with the identification of the needs of society and the endeavour to satisfy those needs by the application of scientific principles and the use of material resources and energy. It is also concerned with solving problems for which there are no right or wrong answers, only good or poor solutions. Technological behaviour requires **activities** that are creative and demanding, where the laws and principles of science, the properties of materials, and the constraints of society and economics, are all applied to the problems of satisfying human needs.

Technological behaviour also involves a variety of **approaches** and **techniques**, such as *systems analysis, problem identification, decision-making, planning, communication of ideas, practical realisation, solution testing* and *evaluation*. It therefore involves considerations other than pure craft and science. The role of people in a technological world, the proper use of technology and its effects on society and the environment, are issues important to us all.

CDT: Technology courses are planned to help pupils gain a better understanding by **doing**, i.e. by getting involved with problems in a practical way. Through experiencing all that is involved in designing and making, knowledge and understanding develop together. **Knowledge** must be acquired for a reason. Then, when it is **applied**, it is fulfilling a purpose. The application of this knowledge will also help deepen your **understanding** of the principles you have learned. So the solving of problems is the *means* by which knowledge and understanding are encouraged to develop in CDT: Technology.

The process of *problem solving* is at the heart of the course and has been adopted as the main *process activity* by all the Examination Groups. To help pupils through a programme of problem solving a *design process* is used; this is treated in detail later in the book. Therefore all pupils will be involved in the following stages:

- Identifying a need, from a situation or context.
- Writing a design brief.
- Analysing the problems.
- Researching and recording data.
- Developing ideas.
- Translating ideas to a material form – modelling.
- Communicating ideas to working drawings.
- Making a product.
- Testing the product against the original need.
- Evaluating the performance of the product against the original need.

Remember you will do well if you enjoy your course and do your best. Success is a partnership between you, your school and the examination course you take. You must work hard, organise, plan and take advice from teachers, parents, and sometimes friends. Your school will provide specialist teachers and equipment to help you. The examination provides a structure around which you can plan and organise your work towards some achievable goals.

The opportunity is there for you to grasp; the fact that you are already reading this book is an indication that you want to do well and it is hoped that you will find the chapters interesting and helpful.

Use the book to tell you more about your examination course and what you can do to be successful. Look at the sample questions and comments; they should help you to improve your work. See how **you** can help by assessing your own work and progress.

Good luck.

5 > ADDRESSES OF THE EXAM GROUPS

University of London Examinations and Assessment Council
ULEAC   Stewart House, 32 Russell Square, London WC1B 5DN

Midland Examining Group
MEG   East Midland Examining Board, Robins Wood House, Robins Wood Road, Aspley, Nottingham NG8 3NR

Northern Examinations and Assessment Board
NEAB   Devas Street, Manchester MI5 6EX

Northern Ireland Schools Examination and Assessment Council
NISEAC   Beechill House, 42 Beechill Road, Belfast BT8 4RS

Southern Examination Group
SEG   Associated Examination Board, Stag Hill House, Guildford, Surrey GU2 5XJ

University of Cambridge Local Examination Syndicate
IGCSE   1 Hills Road, Cambridge CB1 2EU

Welsh Joint Education Committee
WJEC   245 Western Avenue, Cardiff CF5 2YX

HOW TO DO WELL ON THE COURSE

PREPARING FOR THE COURSE

PREPARING FOR THE DESIGN EXAMINATION

PREPARING FOR THE WRITTEN EXAMINATION

PREPARING FOR COURSEWORK

GETTING STARTED

Having chosen to take CDT: Technology as a GCSE subject you naturally want to know what you have to do in order to do well.

Reading the syllabus for your examination will tell you the detail of all you will need to know and how you are going to be assessed. What it will not tell you is how to obtain the best grade possible for the work you have done and the level you have reached. This book will help you to present all of your work in such a way that it will be a true reflection of what you know and what you can do.

Remember that for a GCSE CDT: Technology course, doing well is in **your** hands. Only part of the course is in the form of a formal examination; half of the total marks are for your project(s) and are teacher assessed. Together the examination and assessment provide a means of ensuring that the result you obtain at the end of the course is a fair and accurate assessment of your experience and ability.

ESSENTIAL PRINCIPLES

Your course will have three main areas:

■ Design.

■ Written papers.

■ Coursework – projects.

These are the areas on which you will be assessed during and at the end of your course.

1 **Design** If you take a separate *Design Paper* then it will be sent away to an Examiner for marking. However, if your design assessment is part of your coursework project, then your teacher will assess your work. This assessment is then moderated at the end of the course by the Examining Group.

2 **Written papers** This part of your work is sent away to be marked by an Examiner appointed by the Examining Group.

3 **Coursework** This work is marked by your teacher during and at the end of the course. During the course your teacher will talk to you about how you are doing. This gives you the opportunity to improve your work and your final assessment. Your teacher's assessment is finally moderated by the Examining Group. Usually this means that someone will visit your school and look at some or all of the pupils' coursework.

Now you know how you will be assessed it is important to look at some simple things which **you** can do, to ensure that you achieve the best assessment possible.

1 ▷ PREPARING FOR THE COURSE

If, before you started your GCSE course, you had taken part in a CDT Foundation course you will have a set of notes, design work and some projects. Do not throw these away; they will be useful to you during the GCSE course. They may contain ideas and techniques you will want to use later. They also provide you with a simple means of judging your work; namely, is what you are doing now better than the work you did one or two years ago?

Remember to build up and keep a set of notes for all of your work in Technology. Do not throw away rough design ideas and initial thoughts about a problem. Keep them in a folder with some simple notes to explain what you were trying to do. Keep the work in this folder in order, and use it as a simple ideas resource.

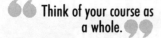

See your course as an integrated whole. In other words, try to avoid thinking that there are separate sections on design, electronics, mechanisms and so on. If you are to do well it is important to be able to use skills and to apply knowledge from different areas of the course. ULEAC and MEG have produced a model to help you see the course as a whole (Fig. 2.1).

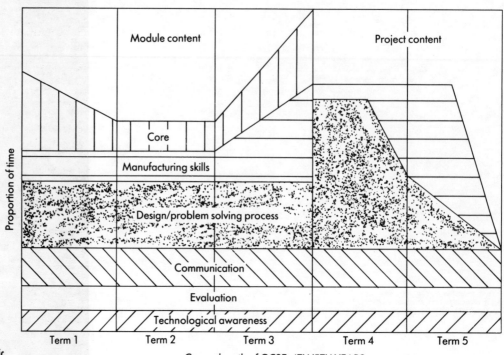

Fig. 2.1 LEAG course schematic

Course length of GCSE 4TH/5TH YEARS

The schematic looks in detail at the final five terms (4th and 5th year) of the GCSE course. Here the particular elements of the CDT: Technology strand are emphasised. However, if students are to be successful it is important that the broad concepts of CDT have been established in an earlier foundation course.

The syllabus should be considered as an integrated unit rather than as a series of unconnected elements. This integrated nature is seen in that some elements of the syllabus appear in all aspects of your work. This is shown in the schematic in elements such as communication, design and the problem solving process. These elements should be emphasised throughout the teaching of the syllabus and can be used as a way of linking the sometimes separate units of knowledge contained in the modules.

So, as you can see from Fig. 2.1 and Fig. 2.2, some aspects of the course are involved in almost everything you do.

A suggested time plan for a two year course

Year one	Common core and design		Module one and design	Module two and design
		Project choice and research		
Year two		Project		
	Revision			
	Examination and project assessment			

Fig. 2.2 MEG course schematic

PREPARING FOR THE DESIGN EXAMINATION

If your course has a design examination you will have an opportunity to research a theme or question *prior* to the formal examination. This will help you to prepare your thoughts so that you are able to answer in detail the questions set in the formal design examination.

These questions will require you to **solve a problem** rather than to be innovative. The examiner is not trying to find out how good an inventor you are, but whether you can apply the design process to the solving of a problem.

You will be expected to use a range of drawing and presentation techniques to **communicate** your ideas. You must also be able to **apply** the technological principles you have learnt, during the core and optional modules, to the solving of the problem.

Chapter 3 looks at Design in more detail.

PREPARING FOR THE WRITTEN EXAMINATION

This consists of two parts:

1   The Core
2   The Optional Modules

The *Core* is a separate paper which you usually take before you do the *Optional Modules*. You take **two** *Optional Modules* which you have chosen at the start of your course.

Each of the Examining Groups has a slightly different style to its written papers, so it is important to check the details of the paper you will be taking. The easiest way to familiarise yourself with the written papers is to look at some past papers from the Examining Group whose syllabus you are taking.

However, there are some general guidelines which you can use to help:

1   Make sure you understand your work. If there is anything you do not understand find out as soon as possible.
2   Revise your work in stages throughout the course.

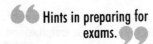

Hints in preparing for exams.

3 Try to reach the point where some of the basic principles you regularly use do not have to be revised.
4 Test yourself to see how much you can remember. It helps to do this as a group.
5 Make a clear plan for your final revision. Start about 12 weeks before the written examination.
6 Look at past papers. Practise answering questions. Sometimes set yourself a time limit. See how much you can do in the same time that you will have in the exam itself.
7 The night before your examination prepare all the things that you need to take into the exam – pens, technical drawing equipment, colours, etc. Then try to relax. Do something which is not connected with CDT:Technology.

Turn to chapters 4 and 6 for more details.

Chapters 4 and 6 look at the written examinations in more detail. They suggest helpful techniques to use in preparing for the exam and give lots of practical material. Chapter 6 also looks at important aspects of the *subject content* you will need to be familiar with in order to achieve 'success'.

4 PREPARING FOR COURSEWORK

Most of the marks are available in this part of the examination. With the exception of the WJEC and NISEC syllabuses you can earn 50% of your marks with one final project. To do well you must thoroughly plan and organise your work over a long period. Usually the final project occupies most of your time during the last three terms of the course.
The following general guidelines will help.

1 Start to think about a project well before you have to start work upon it.
2 Talk to your teacher about your ideas. Try to decide upon a project which you are interested in and which is within your capabilities.

Hints in preparing your coursework.

3 Make sure your project can cover all the assessment objectives in the coursework part of the syllabus.
4 Make sure the amount of work in your project is realistic for the time you have. Remember the other GCSE subjects you are doing will also have a coursework element.
5 Keep a project log to show whether you are keeping up to date with your work.
6 Make sure you know the date that you must finish by. Use your project log to set yourself targets.
7 Do not worry if you cannot finish; providing you have done enough work you can still do well.

Chapter 5 looks at coursework in much more detail. It goes through the vital stages involved in developing your coursework material and in producing the coursework folder. Lots of actual examples are provided together with hints on how you can acquire and develop important techniques for successfully completing a coursework project.

A FINAL STATEMENT

Remember. To do well on the course you need to:

a) be interested in your work;
b) work hard and to the best of your ability in all aspects of the course;
c) accept the advice and guidance of your teacher;
d) complete your work on time for each assessment stage.

DESIGN

GETTING STARTED

Throughout all aspects of your course you will use the *design process*. However, as we have seen earlier, some examining groups set a Design Examination Paper which is conducted under formal examination conditions. In this chapter we will look at the following:

1 The different ways in which you may be asked to use the design process.
2 What the design process is and how you use it.
3 Some of the skills you need.
4 The Design Examination Paper.

It is important that you find out the particular requirements of the examination you are taking.

USING THE DESIGN PROCESS

IDENTIFYING THE NEED

WRITING A DESIGN BRIEF AND SPECIFICATION

ANALYSIS AND RESEARCH

DEVELOPING THE CHOSEN IDEA

MAKING THE DEVELOPED IDEA

EVALUATING THE FINAL PRODUCT

COMMUNICATION SKILLS

YOUR DESIGN FOLIO

ESSENTIAL PRINCIPLES

You can be asked to design in any aspect of the examination. However, exactly what is required will depend upon whether you are answering a question in the *written papers* of the examination, answering a question in the specialist *design paper* or are engaged in the activity of designing your *coursework* final project.

Whenever you design you will have to:

Design requirements.

1 provide a solution, within given criteria, to a problem.
2 record and communicate your ideas and/or solution clearly to others.
3 test and evaluate your solution against the original criteria.

– although not all questions or activities in your course will ask you to use every stage of the process.

If we look at some questions and work from the different aspects of the CDT:Technology assessment we can see how the design requirement changes.

WRITTEN PAPERS

Here we look at some questions on design from the written papers.

Question 1

a) State why it is necessary to have bridges. *(2)*

b) Draw a simple example of **each** of the following types of bridge:
  i) beam;
  ii) cantilever;
  iii) arch;
  iv) suspension. *(8)*

c) Faced with the problem of designing a bridge over a river, list **six** factors that need to be considered in the design. *(10)*

(WJEC)

This question is part of the common core paper. Here you are only dealing with one aspect of design; the examiner is asking you to set the criteria for the design brief of the bridge. You must consider what factors are important when designing a bridge to span a river.

Question 2

Fig. 3.1 shows the outline shape of a tray which will be used to serve snack meals. The tray is to be vacuum formed from 1 mm PVC sheet.

a) State two ways in which the tray might distort in use.

Answer i): _____

_____

Answer ii): _____

_____ *(9)*

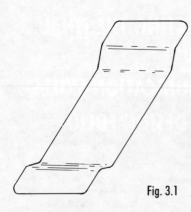

Fig. 3.1

b) The tray is to be redesigned with recesses for a glass, a plate and cutlery. Fig. 3.2 shows three possible arrangements for these recesses.

State which of these arrangements would give:

i) the stiffest tray: _____ *(1)*

ii) the most flexible tray: _____ *(1)*

iii) Give one reason for your choice of the stiffest arrangement.

Answer: _____

_____

_____ *(1)*

(SEG (part))

Fig. 3.2

Again, this is a question from the common core. In this question you are being asked to show your familiarity with several aspects of the design process as well as your knowledge of materials and structures. In parts a) and b) you are having to give a simple evaluation of the design of the tray. Part c) below requires you to provide a solution which will further improve the design. You are not expected to provide a range of alternative solutions at this stage. One possible idea, which is clearly communicated, is sufficient, as in the suggested answer below.

c) Show by means of a sketch how the section of the tray could be changed to make further improvements to the stiffness. (2)

(SEG (part))

_____

_____

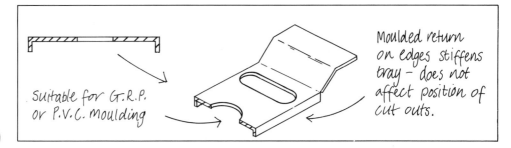

Fig. 3.3 Student answer to part c)

Often the depth of answer required can be judged by looking at the *mark value* of the question. Parts (d) and (e) below, **together** give only 2 marks, so clearly brief answers only are required. The **space available** in the answer booklets is another good guide to what is expected of you.

d) State **two** other general factors which the designer should consider when planning this tray.

Factor i) _____

_____

Factor ii) _____

_____

e) State one advantage and one disadvantage of making this tray from glass reinforced plastic (GRP) rather than from PVC.

Advantage: _____

Disadvantage: _____ (2)

(SEG (part))

Part (d), like the WJEC question, is again asking you to provide criteria for the *design brief* of the tray. Part (e) tests your knowledge of the properties of various materials, and your ability to apply that knowledge to a particular situation.

In the written paper you will not be asked to go through the complete design process. However, you will have to show that you can use various parts of the process. You can expect to be asked to:

What the written paper tests.

1   Analyse and produce criteria for a design brief.
2   Provide simple solutions or modify a given design so that some properties are improved.
3   Evaluate a given design or several alternative designs. Sometimes this will be a general evaluation, at other times, as in the SEG question, you will be asked to evaluate the designs against certain criteria.

DESIGN PAPERS

Will you take a Design Paper?

If you are taking a syllabus which uses a design paper you will have two parts to your design examination. The first part of the examination is a *preparation paper* which allows you to research information about a theme or broad question. Here we illustrate by using the MEG paper which gives you a range of themes which you can research.

MIDLAND EXAMINING GROUP   1451/1(T)
General Certificate of Secondary Education

CDT – TECHNOLOGY
PAPER 1 DESIGN PAPER – THEMES
To be given to candidates on or after Monday 23rd May 1988

The paper will contain six questions of which you will be required to answer one.

The Themes relating to each of the Questions are as follows:

1.   *Use of computers by the disabled.*

2.   *Vehicle steering checks.*

3.   *Stirring aids for cooks.*

4.   *Litter collection.*

5.   *Television quiz game indicator.*

6.   *Sorting devices.*

Information collected during your preparation for the examination must **not** *be taken into the examination room.*

LEAG give you more detailed questions from which you choose one to research. You can see an example of such a question below.

OUTLINE SITUATIONS

Pre Examination Considerations

1.   Very often in schools computers are used in a range of teaching and learning situations. This means that the computer, and its associated hardware, has to be moved around the corridors of the school and then wheeled into a room where pupils will sit and use it.

You have been asked to investigate the problem as a solution is required to be made in the school workshops. You are told that, with the increasing use teachers are making of the equipment, specially designed rooms are constantly in use and other rooms must be brought into service. One such room is up a small flight of stairs.

The normal computer set-up consists of:

A BBC Master computer,
A double disc drive,
A metal-cased monitor,
A standard printer.

Investigate the problem with the intention of designing some mobile form of storage/workplace.

Both of these papers allow you to research and investigate in order to prepare information which will help you in your formal design examination. In the MEG examination you are not allowed to take your research into the examination with you. However, the LEAG examination does allow you to take the work you have put on the pre-printed examination sheets into the formal design examination.

Fig. 3.4 provides an example of the pre-exam work which one candidate produced for the LEAG design examination, which has been slightly amended for the purposes of this book. The candidate was looking at the design problems of moving a computer system about a school and up some stairs.

> ❝Pre-exam work can be vital.❞

Fig. 3.4 Student work on preparation paper (LEAG)

From the outlined Solution 1 I have predicted that a mobile/storage trolley for a computer system must be designed which complies with the following Specification:

1) It must move along flat corridors, through doorways and up a small flight of stairs.
2) It must hold a BBC master, double disc drive, printer and monitor securely and safely and allow access to power sockets.
3) It must allow air to circulate to prevent over heating.
4) It must be robust to cope with transportation but lightweight enough to be carried and be made using materials and methods of production all possible in a workshop.
5) It must have a method of adjusting the height of the keyboard to make it most comfortable to use.
   + possibly having a locking system for security and a cover to stop dust collecting.
   + keep the system as cheap as possible without detracting from the functioning.

TYPICAL DIMENSIONS

Behind all pieces of equipment are the connecting and power leads.

There are two different types of d-disk drive.

BBC MASTER

It is also advisable to leave space around the computer for add-ons and around all equipment to allow air to circulate to prevent over-heating.

BBC MONITOR

BBC D-DISC DRIVE

PRINTER

The printers compatible with the BBC are numerous but they are all of the same order of magnitude. These are typical dimensions.
W. 360mm D. 300mm H. 140mm

For the trolley to fit the specification it will have to run through corridors, through doors, up stairs and be stable and safe. I have measured the smallest door that I think the trolley will have to go through.

Sources of Research
- School computer equipment.
- my own measurements.
- photographs I took of a computer trolley.
- Beebug computer magazine (for BBC).

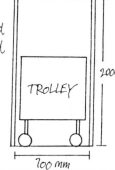
TROLLEY

700 mm

2000mm

ERGONOMIC DATA OF TROLLEY

If the total dimensions are such that it would not fit through the door the trolley may have to have a collapsible part.

ERGONOMICS OF USER

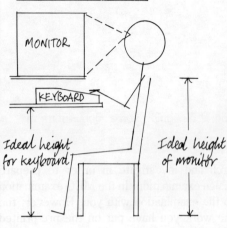

MONITOR

KEYBOARD

Ideal height for keyboard

Ideal height of monitor

From investigation I have discovered that the range of adjustability needs to be as follows.

Height of monitor	Height of keyboard
max 1200mm	max 850mm
min 900mm	min 550mm
Range 300mm	Range 300mm

This should cater for children from 11+ to adult who are of average height. It shows that the height of both monitor and keyboard can be made together and not independently.

LEGROOM

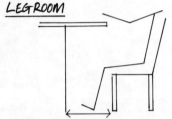

To give comfortable legroom there needs to be a clearance of approx 400mm.

EXISTING BBC COMPUTER TROLLEYS.

Right are two examples of currently available trolleys for the BBC computer but also for the master. Features to notice are the stacking. They both have the computer directly below the monitor and the disc-drive to the right-hand side. Neither secure the equipment down to the shelves.

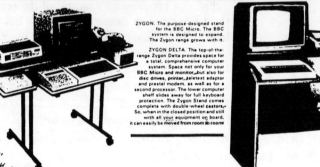

ZYGON. The purpose-designed stand for the BBC Micro. The BBC system is designed to expand. The Zygon range grows with it.

ZYGON DELTA. The top-of-the-range Zygon Delta provides space for a total, comprehensive computer system. Space not only for your BBC Micro and monitor, but also for disc drives, printer, teletext adaptor and prestel modem, as well as for a second processor. The lower computer shelf slides away for full keyboard protection. The Zygon Stand comes complete with double-wheel castors. So, when in the closed position and still with all your equipment on board, it can easily be moved from room to room!

MATERIAL SELECTION

As mentioned in the analysis the trolley must have high-tensile strength to cope with the heavy equipment but must also be light for transportation up a flight of stairs. Factors to be taken account of when choosing materials: - properties and suitability - cost - durability - easy to clean.

WOOD

Plywood - relatively expensive, very strong.
Chipboard - very cheap.
Blockboard - relatively expensive, very strong.
Hardwood - cheap, good finish.

FIBRES

Medium density Fibre board
- very cheap very strong
- can spray paint finish
- as heavy as plywood
could be useful.

METAL - useful forms of steel

Ø5-50mm - rod-

5-50mm - square-

W12-50mm - flat-
T1.5-6mm

Ø5-40mm - tube-

12-25mm square tube

50x25mm rectangle (one size) tube

angle

+ Stainless steel (very expensive, good finish)

LOCKS + COVERS

The best lock seems to be a simple padlock.

A possible cover could be a tambar. This can be seen on a shop window when its closed.

steel straps on a material back.

Remember. In the preparation part of the design examination you will have to:

1 Research and analyse a variety of information about a theme or broad question.
2 Communicate this information in a clear and concise way. You can use drawings, notes, paste-up techniques etc.

In the second part of the design examination you will have a more detailed question to answer. We now look at some examples of this more detailed type of question in the second part of the design paper.

The examples from the MEG and LEAG examinations show you the type of question which is asked and how it relates to the theme or broad question given in the preparation paper. Now you will have to answer this question under formal examination conditions.

Examples: MEG

1 A person suffering from a stiffness of the finger joints has difficulty in typing on a computer keyboard, as shown in Fig. 3.5. Design a device which will enable this person to input information to a computer more easily. *(40)*

Fig. 3.5

2 The front wheels of a motor vehicle need to be adjusted so that the **track**, as shown in Fig. 3.6, is set to the correct toe in, toe out, or parallel, according to the manufacturer's recommendation.

For toe in, dimension b will be greater than dimension a by the specified amount, usually no more than 5 mm difference.

For toe out, dimension a will be greater than dimension b.

For parallel tracking, the dimensions a and b will be the same.

Design a device to enable a person to check the track of a motor car accurately. *(40)*

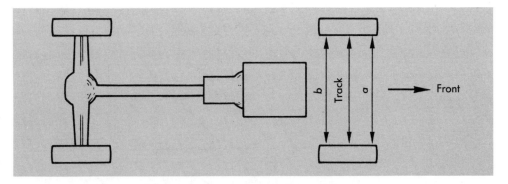

Fig. 3.6

3 A cook has difficulty in stirring the contents of more than one saucepan at a time, which is often necessary when preparing a meal. Design a device which will enable the contents of a saucepan to be stirred automatically. *(40)*

4 A town council is concerned about the amount of litter lying in its paved shopping precinct. Design a device to enable a person patrolling the precinct during shopping hours to collect the litter hygienically. *(40)*

5 In a television quiz game, the quizmaster needs to know which contestant is ready to answer the question first. Design a device which will indicate the first of the three contestants to be ready to answer. *(40)*

6 A mixed batch of wooden beads, as shown in Fig. 3.7, are to be painted in different colours, according to their size. The 20 mm diameter beads are to be blue, the 15 mm diameter beads red, and the 10 mm diameter beads green. Design a device which will sort the beads from a chute, and channel them to the correct paint tank.   *(40)*

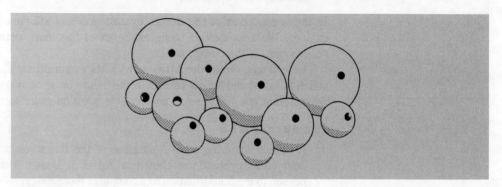

Fig. 3.7

Example : LEAG

Very often school computers are used in a range of situations. This means that the computer and its associated hardware has to be moved around the corridors of the school and then wheeled into a room where pupils will sit and use it.

The normal computer set-up consists of

	(Width	× Depth	× Height)
A BBC Master computer, size	450	× 350	× 75 mm
A double disc drive, size	300	× 350	× 70 mm
A metal-cased monitor, size	350	× 350	× 350 mm
A standard printer, size	400	× 350	× 200 mm

Pupils need to have the keyboard at a working height of 800 mm.

The corridors of the school are perfectly wide and adequate to push the computer set-up about. However, the class-room is up THREE steps. The height of each step is 200 mm and the depth 300 mm (see Fig. 3.8).

You may assume that a technician will fix the computer equipment permanently to your design and complete all the electrical work.

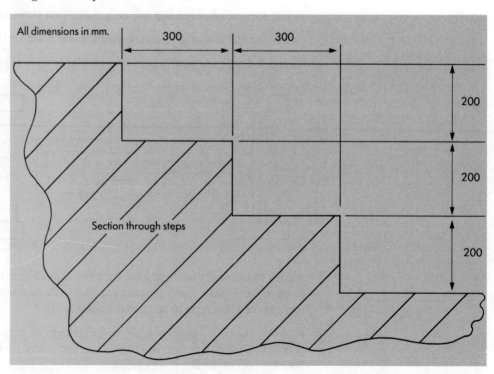

Fig. 3.8 The section through the steps

Design some mobile form of storage/workplace which can accommodate the computer set-up and can be used by the pupils in all the rooms of the school. Your design should be capable of being made in a school workshop.

You will have to answer such questions under formal examination conditions. For this type of question you will have to:

- identify the need.
- determine the design brief.
- analyse the problems.
- develop a range of ideas.
- evaluate and make critical judgements about these ideas.
- determine a final solution.
- present a working or final drawing of your solution.
- evaluate your solution against the original criteria.

66 Be ready to discuss these in your answer. **99**

You will **not** have to:

- model your ideas.
- make your solution.
- test your solution.

The two design papers below show you some actual examples of student work, together with some examiner's comments.

STUDENT ANSWERS WITH EXAMINER COMMENTS

Fig. 3.9 Student work on meat cutter problem

1 Proposed solutions to a meat cutter problem.

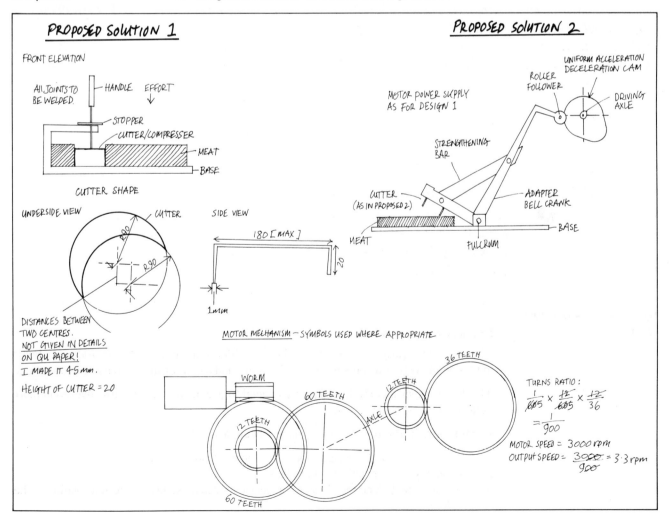

Examiner comment

Clear sketches showing two possible solutions to the problem. Some use of shading, though more could have been displayed. Dimensions are shown, together with speed calculations. There is a need for some pictorial views to be given.

2   Alarm systems for store security.

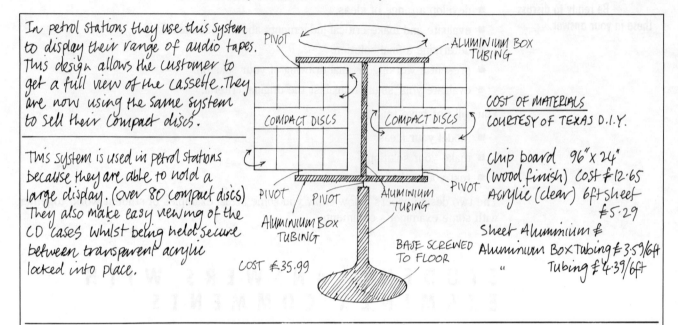

In petrol stations they use this system to display their range of audio tapes. This design allows the customer to get a full view of the cassette. They are now using the same system to sell their compact discs.

This system is used in petrol stations because they are able to hold a large display. (over 80 compact discs) They also make easy viewing of the CD cases whilst being held secure between transparent acrylic locked into place.

PIVOT

ALUMINIUM BOX TUBING

COMPACT DISCS

COMPACT DISCS

PIVOT   PIVOT   PIVOT

Aluminium Box TUBING

Aluminium TUBING

BASE SCREWED TO FLOOR

COST £35.99

COST OF MATERIALS
COURTESY OF TEXAS D.I.Y.

Chip board 96" x 24"
(wood finish) Cost £12.65
Acrylic (clear) 6ft sheet
£5.29

Sheet Aluminium £
Aluminium Box Tubing £3.59/6ft
     "   Tubing £4.39/6ft

SECURITY

Alarms are a major part of store security. At the moment, music shops and other places that sell records, tapes and compact discs, like woolworths use bugs which are clipped inside the casings or they are hidden under the price tags themselves. Here are some examples.

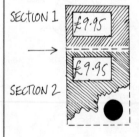

SECTION 1 £9.95

SECTION 2 £9.95

This alarm is in the form of a sticker similar to a price tag. A flat bugging device is placed under the sticker; the sticker is then stuck on the article for sale. When a customer buys the article, they take it to the counter where the sales assistant removes section 2 containing the bug.

ALARM SYSTEMS	
ADVANTAGES	DISADVANTAGES
Reduces loss in stocks due to theft. discourages theft. Can be re-used time and time again.	In the event of power cut they are rendered useless. Can discourage customers. Cost lots of money to install and maintain.

Fig. 3.10 Student work on alarm systems

Examiner comments

The work is clearly divided up to show the different areas being considered. Some indication of costing has been given. Also some indication of the sources of information.

The design paper and the techniques you need to use in answering it are covered in more detail at the end of this chapter.

Remember. In the design paper you are being asked to show:

1   Your ability to use the design process to solve a problem logically.
2   Your ability to communicate your ideas.
3   The reasoning behind the choices and decisions you make in arriving at a solution to the problem.

COURSEWORK

In your final coursework project, and in any mini projects which form part of your coursework, you will have to make full use of the *design process* (see below). It is important that you:

- Try to apply the process in a logical way and clearly show how you have arrived at decisions.
- Always communicate your ideas in a clear and concise way.

    Chapter 5 will look at coursework in more detail.

STAGES IN THE DESIGN PROCESS

There are many different models of the design process ranging from very simple linear models to more complex models with feed-back loops such as that shown in Fig. 3.11.

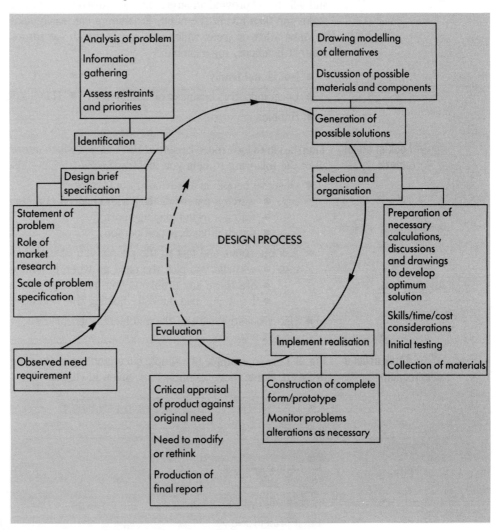

Fig. 3.11 The design process (MEG example)

 We now look at the design process in more detail.

Your teacher may use one particular model to help you understand the design process. It does not matter which model is used; what is important is that you realise that the model gives you a logical sequence of stages to follow. These stages start with the identification of a need, and lead through to the evaluation of a solution. All of the models have these stages in common.

As a method or approach this process is accepted by all of the Examination Groups. Whichever syllabus you are taking you will need to show your ability in:

- identifying a need;
- writing a design brief and specification;
- analysis and research;
- considering a number of potential ideas;
- developing the chosen idea;
- making the developed idea – realisation;
- evaluating the final product to see how well it meets the original need.

Stages in the design process

Now we will look in detail at what you have to do at each stage of the process.

2 IDENTIFYING THE NEED

Once you can *identify a need* you are on the way to having a problem which can be solved. Usually you have to identify the need from a broad context or situation, although sometimes the need is provided for you. For example, in the examinations which use a design paper, the broad context is given in the pre-examination paper, and the more detailed need is provided by the questions in the formal design examination.

You must identify a need.

In your coursework *you* have to provide the need. It is important to start thinking about this at an early stage in your course. Try to think of something which is of interest to you and which will provide an interesting and worthwhile project. Do not choose something to make and *then* invent the need. Examiners can easily spot this.

Make a list of areas which you can research for **ideas**; at this stage use very broad context headings, for example:

- Home and family
- Local industry, business or commerce
- Hobbies
- Sport
- Handicapped

Look at actual contexts.

Then begin to look more closely at the *contexts* which interest you most. Consider some or all of the following to help you identify a *need* from a chosen context.

- Observe people in a particular context,
  - e.g. • watch a parent dealing with children in a family.
    - watch a friend playing sport.
    - watch a handicapped person.

Observe.

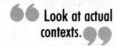

- Ask questions and talk to the people you observe,
  - e.g. • why did you pick the child up when he started to cry?
    - are there any problems you have with your sports kit?
    - I saw you had difficulty holding the vegetables you were preparing?

Ask questions.

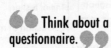

- Use a questionnaire to try and identify problems.

Think about a questionnaire.

Fig. 3.12 is an example of a simple questionnaire of the type you could use to help identify a problem. Some more examples are given in chapter 5.

	AMOUNT OF DIFFICULTY				COMMENT
QUESTIONS	Not a problem			Very difficult	
Do you find it difficult to stand up?	✓				
or sit down?	✓				
Is it difficult to hold things?				✓	
to turn the pages of a book?				✓	
to turn door handles?			✓		
Can you add any more questions?					

Fig. 3.12 Use of questionnaire for the handicapped

Make a list of some things which you think might help **solve** some of the problems you have observed. At this point the 'solutions' need not be too detailed – we are only using **this** list to generate further discussion to help us identify the **need** more precisely.

Ask the people you observed if any of your 'solutions' would be useful. Then use this and all the other information you have gathered to identify a particular need.

Remember. Identifying the need:

- is the starting point of the design process.
- usually takes much longer than you expect.

3 ▷ WRITING A DESIGN BRIEF AND SPECIFICATION

Having identified the need you are now in a position to say exactly **how** you will try to meet it. This is called a *design brief*. Whenever we design we start with a design brief, which says what it is we are going to try to do. The example in Fig. 3.13 shows how a candidate has produced a design brief for a CDT: Technology project, from an identified need. The design brief must set out the broad criteria for what it is you are trying to do.

Start with a design brief.

I am going to design and make a multi-purpose aid for holding things. It is intended to be used by my granny who has arthritis and has great difficulty in holding knives, forks, turning pages, etc.

It must be able to hold :
knives
forks
It must be able to be adapted to hold:
a device for turning pages
a device for opening door handles e.g

Fig. 3.13 Student design brief for handicapped project

At this stage it is better to allow some room for changes to be made. If the brief is very specific you may not be able to use some very good ideas which come to you at a later stage.

I intend to make an automatic porch light system. It will work by using an electronic circuit with a photocell for sensing the light level and a two stage transistor circuit for amplification. The light will be switched by the use of a mains relay. The circuit will be boxed in a weatherproof plastic case.

Fig. 3.14 Example of too specific a design brief

Fig. 3.14 shows a design brief that was much too tight. The candidate has said how the problem will be solved **before** attempting any investigation or research and before looking at any possible solutions. Remember, the design brief is only the starting point – not the beginning **and** the finish.

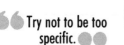 Try not to be too specific.

When you write a brief for your final project it is helpful to see it in two stages.

1 A main part which you know you can do in the time available.
2 An additional part which can be achieved if you have enough time.

In the following examples, Fig. 3.15 and Fig. 3.16, you can see how two different candidates have done just this.

Example one: design brief for automatic lighting system

> I am going to design an automatic lighting system for the outside of my house. I want the system to switch on when it becomes dark.
>
> When I have got the basic system working I will try to link it to the burglar alarm system, so that it will trigger the alarm if an intruder is present.

Fig. 3.15 Design brief for automatic lighting system

Examiner comment

This brief has been divided into two clear areas.

1   The development and making of an automatic lighting system.
2   The linking of that system, when working, with a burglar alarm system.

This has the advantage that if the candidate experiences problems on the development of the lighting system, the project can be easily modified to become just a lighting system.

Example two: design brief for rucksack frame

> For my final project I am going to design a lightweight rucksack frame, for use when I go camping with the venture scouts.
>
> If possible I want to make the frame so that it is a knock down structure for storage.

Fig. 3.16 Design brief for lightweight rucksack frame

Examiner comment

This brief, as with the previous one, has two clear areas.

1   The development of a lightweight rucksack frame.
2   The production of a knock down design.

Again, the candidate has allowed two routes for the development of the project. If the basic design of a lightweight frame becomes time consuming or very difficult then the 'knock down' concept can be left undone.

SPECIFICATION

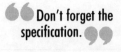 **Don't forget the specification.**

As well as the design brief you will need a full *specification*. It is important particularly in the coursework part of the examination to have a specification as well as your design brief.

- The *design brief* is a broad statement of intent – it is what you will try to do.
- The *specification* is the specific detail – it is the clear limits and targets you will work to.

> I am going to design an automatic lighting system for the outside of my house. I want the system to switch on when it becomes dark.

> When I have got the basic system working I will try to link it to the burglar alarm system, so that it will trigger the alarm if an intruder is present.
>
> Specification:
>
> 1) The system must switch on at a set light level. This level must be adjustable.
> 2) The system must have an over-ride on/off switch.
> 3) The System must be able to interface with the 240 volt A.C. house lighting System.
> 4) The outside parts must be weatherproof.
> 5) It will probably be electronic.
> 6) It must sense an intruder who is within 3 metres of the house.
> 7) The intruder parts of the system must have a manual override
> 8) The System needs to cost no more than £20.

Fig. 3.17 Design brief and specification for automatic lighting system

Examiner comment

Here (Fig. 3.17) the candidate has begun to set out the detailed specification from the design brief. You can see how some targets and limits have been provided.

Often you cannot complete the specification until you have carried out some analysis and research. However, it is a good idea to try writing a simple specification once you have written a design brief, even if you change some of the detail or add more after analysing and researching a problem.

The specification should contain:

- specific details of what you will try to do;
- some idea of the material limitations you will have;
- some outline of the techniques to be used, e.g. electronics/mechanical;
- the cost limitations you will work to;
- some consideration of the time limits involved.

 **Aspects of the specification.**

Writing the design brief and specification is one of the most important steps in the design process because, when you have finished, it is what you will **evaluate** your final solution against.

Remember. Writing the design brief and specification is when:

- you clearly say what it is you are going to try to do.
- you take into consideration the limitations and restrictions on time, materials and cost that you will have to work to.
- you set out the criteria or standards by which your finished design or product is to be tested and evaluated.

As we have indicated, they may not happen at the same time; the specification might be completed **after** the analysis and research stage.

4 ANALYSIS AND RESEARCH

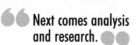 **Next comes analysis and research.**

Having said what it is you will try to do, it is now necessary to look more closely at the areas you have decided to research, to help find ideas to solve the problem. It is important to remember that most ideas do not occur as magic flashes of inspiration but as the result of logical and methodical analysis and research. However, at this stage it is a good idea to take one sheet of paper and to write down or sketch anything that occurs to you about the problem. This part of the analysis and research process is called a *brainstorm* (Fig. 3.18).

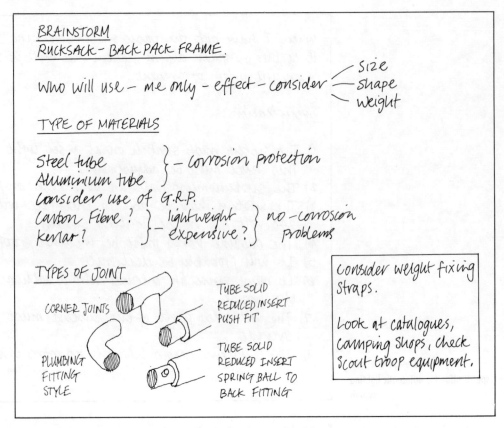

Fig. 3.18 Brainstorming approach
for rucksack frame

66 **Brainstorming can be
useful.** 99

When you have completed the brainstorm you will have a series of *questions* which you
may need to research further. Some of these questions will be general to all problems;
others will be specific to the particular problem you are solving. Fig. 3.19 outlines the
categories into which many of your questions may fall.

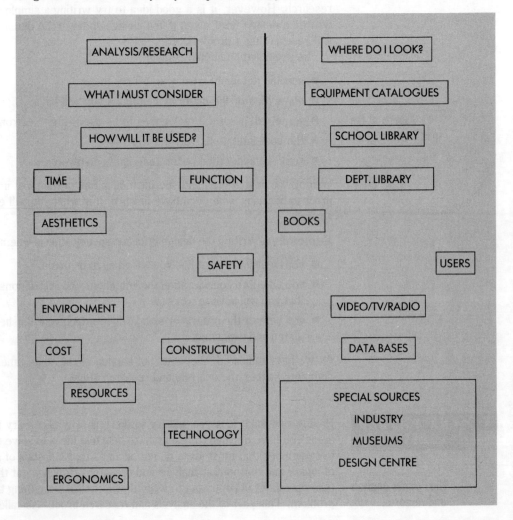

Fig. 3.19 Issues for further
consideration in your analysis and
research

Some of the things you must consider are as follows. Remember that you may have provided answers to some of them in your design brief; or the answers may already be part of your specification. The categories are not in any order and should have equal importance in your thinking.

Technology
- Is the technology you will use appropriate to the product or need?
- Can you make it work?
- How will you make it work?

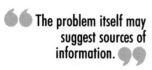
Categories into which your questions might be grouped.

Materials
- Which ones will you use?
- Are they available?
- Are they suitable for the need?
- What will they cost?

Resources
- What resources are available?
- What skills and knowledge do you have?
- What new things do you need to learn?

Cost
- How much will the design cost?
- Is the cost acceptable?

Function
- How must the design work?

Aesthetics
- How will the design appear?

Ergonomics
- Is it the right shape?
- Is it the right size?
- Who will use it?

Safety
- Is it going to be safe to use?
- Are there any safety factors which must be designed in?

Construction
- How can it be made?

Environment
- Will the design have any environmental effect – in use – while being made?

Time
- Is it feasible to do, in the time available?

These categories are applicable to any problem which you consider.

Sources of information

Once you have decided what things you must consider, where do you start to search for *information*? Here there can be an almost endless list. Often the problem provides some suitable starting points.

The problem itself may suggest sources of information.

In the example below you are shown a question from a LEAG design paper. It is fairly easy to list some of the possible research sources.

On Saturdays you work in the local record shop as a Sales Assistant. Part of your job is to unpack the new deliveries and put them out for display. It is necessary to keep an accurate record of what arrives and what is sold, the rest should be in stock.

It becomes obvious that many of the compact-discs are being stolen by shop-lifters. The owner decides to put only the cases out on display and to get the assistants to put the discs into the cases when they are sold.

After a while even this seems not to be working! You hear that even empty cases are a status symbol for some people and they will go to almost any lengths to obtain them.

In desperation the owner comes to you knowing of your technological skills and asks you to help him. He thinks that a display holding the compact-disc boxes securely is needed but that the customers will not like it. You suggest that what is needed is something that the customers will enjoy looking at and which will involve them in choosing their discs. A storage system with some form of control for the customers to operate it, preferably with some movement, is what they would like. Then they would look at the display, choose their disc, read off a code and ask for it at the counter.

This seems like a good idea. Investigate the problem so that when you next meet the owner you have an outline system to discuss with him.

(LEAG)

Comment

You can often begin to identify research sources by reading through a question and highlighting some of the main points, as in the example above.

- Local record shop. This is your first possible source. Other record shops can be further sources of information.
- Accurate record of what is sold. How do the shops keep records? Do they use bar codes? Can this be useful?
- Stolen by shop-lifters. Consider the local police crime-prevention officer. Look at precautions taken in shops.
- Holding compact discs securely. Look at methods of holding/displaying discs.
- Enjoy looking at. Do a customer survey. What do they like doing? How do they like choosing goods?
- Control. Do an investigation on control. Look at moving shop displays.

As with the analysis, whatever the particular question, it is always a good idea to consider some or all of the following sources.

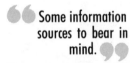 **Some information sources to bear in mind.**

Users

- Talk to people who will use what you are designing.
- Talk to people who already use similar products or systems to the one you are designing.

Magazines, books, video, information technology

- Look in the school and local library or CDT department library for information.
- Use videos/TV and radio programmes as a possible source of information. Sometimes the CDT department or school library has a selection you can use.
- Use databases as a source of information. These can be both local to your school or national such as NERIS, PROFILE, TTNS.

Manufacturers

Talk to and obtain literature from manufacturers or shops which sell products similar to the one you are designing.

Specialised information

Often specific information can be obtained from establishments such as The Design Centre, Museums, Industrial Institutes, etc.

Your research needs to be very wide and to use as many sources as possible. Remember you must **record** all the information you gain; it is also essential that you **acknowledge** the source of your information. In both design papers and coursework, examiners will be looking for the acknowledgement of research sources as a means of judging the range of your research work.

In Fig. 3.20 you can see how a candidate has analysed a problem and shown several research sources as part of a design paper.

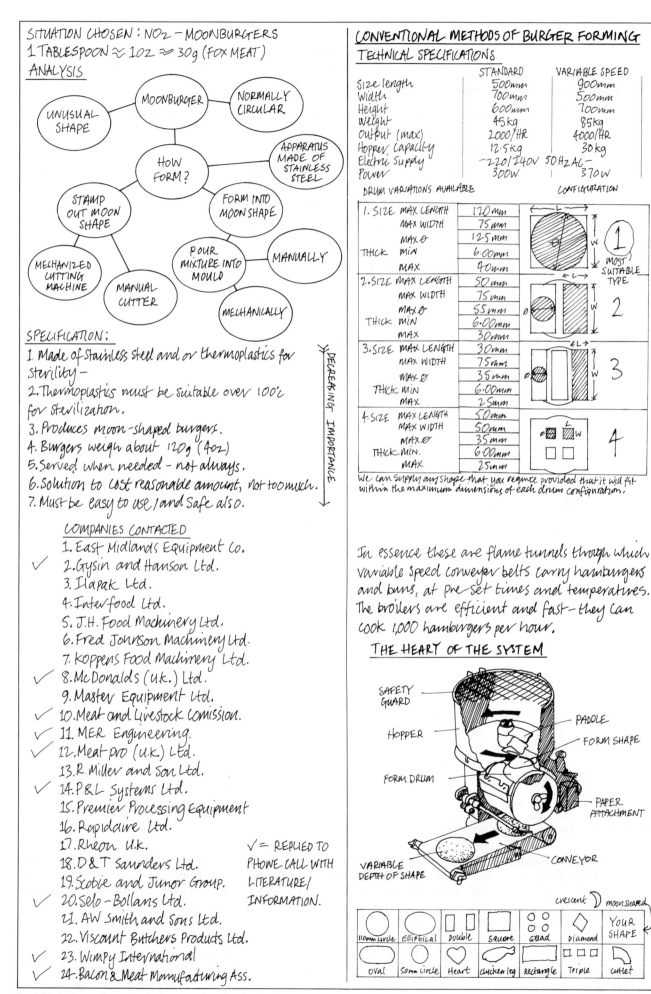

Fig. 3.20 Analysis and sources of information for a fast food problem

Examiner comment

This candidate has used a variety of catalogues as an initial source of information. She has also visited shops and written to a variety of companies to gain information.

Remember. Analysis and research is:

- looking at a problem methodically and in a logical order, and not about getting magic ideas from somewhere.
- helped by starting with a brainstorm sheet to raise some ideas and questions.
- only valid if it is properly recorded and acknowledges the sources from which information was gained.
- about looking widely at a problem. The information you gain must, finally, be presented as a précis of the essential factors necessary to help develop your design ideas.

DEVELOPING POTENTIAL IDEAS

Now you are ready to start to **develop** your own solutions to the problem. Use the essential factors from your analysis and research to help you. Sometimes it helps to look at **specific aspects** of the problem. In the example (Fig. 3.21) you can see how a candidate has looked at aspects of a problem before trying to provide a whole solution.

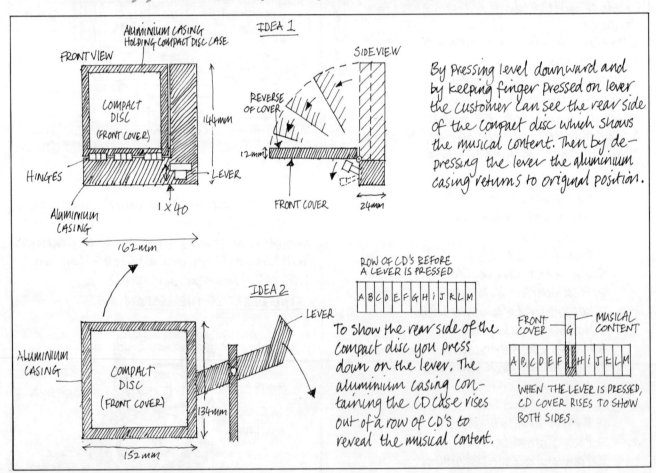

Fig. 3.21 Breaking a problem down into various aspects

Once you have considered aspects of the problem and provided some ideas, you must look at the solution **as a whole**. It is also important at this stage to refer to your design brief and specification to ensure that your solutions are meeting the original standards or criteria. Often candidates lose marks by producing solutions which do **not** meet the criteria of the design brief.

Look at the problem on computer mobility (Fig. 3.22).

It is a good idea to try to produce about three *alternative solutions* at this stage. You will have a chance of gaining higher marks if your alternatives show *different approaches* to the problem rather than being just variations of one idea. However, all of your solutions must be relevant to the design brief.

Very often in schools computers are used in a range of situations. This means that the computer and its associated hardware has to be moved around the corridors of the school and then wheeled into a room where pupils will sit and use it.

The normal computer set-up consists   (Width × Depth × Height)

A BBC Master computer, size   450 × 350 × 75 mm
A double disc drive, size   300 × 350 × 70 mm
A metal-cased monitor, size   350 × 350 × 350 mm
A standard printer, size   400 × 350 × 200 mm

Pupils need to have the keyboard at a working height of 800 mm.

The corridors of the school are perfectly wide and adequate to push the computer set-up about. However, the class-room is up THREE steps. The height of each step is 200 mm and the depth 300 mm. (See Figure)

You may assume that a technician will fix the computer equipment permanently to your design and complete all the electrical work.

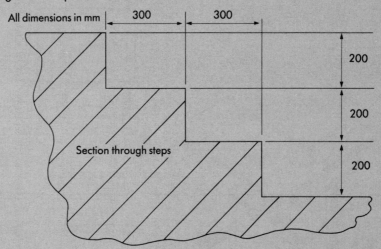

Design some mobile form of storage/workplace which can accommodate the computer set-up and can be used by the pupils in all the rooms of the school. Your design should be capable of being made in a school workshop.

Fig. 3.22 Problem on computer mobility

In particular, when you are doing coursework, this is the stage when you should make use of mock-ups and models to help develop your ideas. You should consider using some of the following.

> **Mock-ups can help.**

- Kit systems – technical Lego, Fischertechnic, Meccano, electronics systems, pneumatic systems – to model parts of an idea.
- Card, balsa, polystyrene and corruflute sheet to produce 3 dimensional and 2 dimensional models.

All of your work in producing potential ideas must be **recorded**. Most of this will be in the form of notes and sketches but you can use photographs, models, paste-ups from catalogues, tape or video-recordings, etc. However, you must also note the advantages and disadvantages of each idea and give the **reasons** for choosing one idea, or parts of several ideas, to continue as your final design. This **justification** of your choice is most important and one of the areas which is missed out by many candidates.

> **Reasons behind your choice must be given.**

Remember. Potential ideas are:
- When you begin to develop your own alternative solutions to the problem.
- Only valid if they are relevant to the original design brief and specification.
- Only useful when properly recorded with their advantages and disadvantages.
- What you use to develop the final design. Examiners must see the justification for your choice.

5   DEVELOPING THE CHOSEN IDEA

Once you have produced some **potential** ideas, you need to make a reasoned choice of which idea or which parts of several ideas you will develop as your **final idea** or design. It is important that you demonstrate some **development** in your idea rather than just take a potential idea as the final design.

You must now begin to provide detailed information on the final design. You will need to provide the following.

■ Detailed drawings showing dimensions and materials to be used.

- Details of construction.
- Sequence of construction.
- A work schedule for coursework projects.

Aspects of the final design.

It is important, of course, that **you** understand your final design and how it will be made. But it is still more important that **other people**, including the examiner, are given enough information to understand how it is to be made.

The student example below (Fig. 3.23) is on the right lines, giving information and explanation, though it has missed out some important aspects of the design brief.

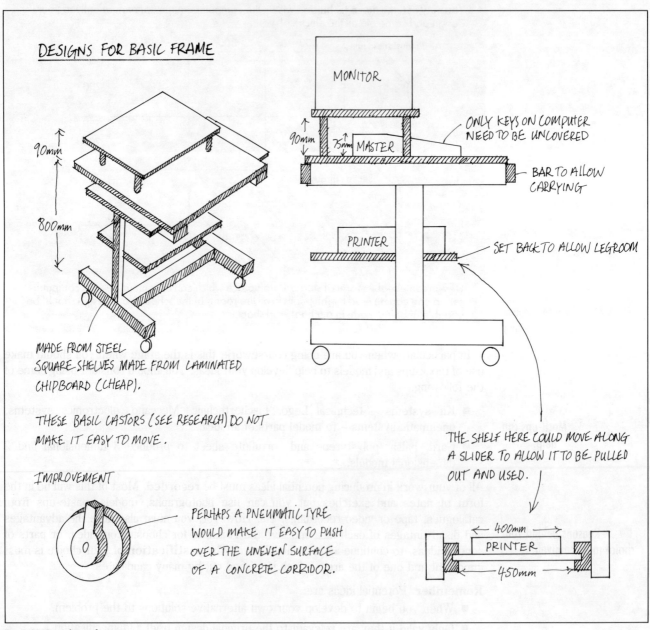

DESIGNS FOR BASIC FRAME

MONITOR

90mm

800mm

MADE FROM STEEL
SQUARE SHELVES MADE FROM LAMINATED
CHIPBOARD (CHEAP).

THESE BASIC CASTORS (SEE RESEARCH) DO NOT
MAKE IT EASY TO MOVE.

IMPROVEMENT

PERHAPS A PNEUMATIC TYRE
WOULD MAKE IT EASY TO PUSH
OVER THE UNEVEN SURFACE
OF A CONCRETE CORRIDOR.

90mm 25mm MASTER

ONLY KEYS ON COMPUTER
NEED TO BE UNCOVERED

BAR TO ALLOW
CARRYING

PRINTER

SET BACK TO ALLOW LEGROOM

THE SHELF HERE COULD MOVE ALONG
A SLIDER TO ALLOW IT TO BE PULLED
OUT AND USED.

← 400mm →
PRINTER
450mm

Fig. 3.23 Providing information about what you are doing

Examiner comment

This solution, whilst being good for housing the computer system, has not considered the main aspect of the problem. Namely, how the trolley will be able to go up a small flight of stairs.

Remember. Developing the chosen idea is about communicating your final design in detail so it can be made. Keep going back to the brief and specification to check that you are doing what is required.

6 > MAKING THE DEVELOPED IDEA

66 Realisation is more important in coursework! 99

This is where you now *realise* or *make* what you have designed. You only fully deal with this aspect of the process in your coursework. We therefore look at this in more detail in chapter 5, 'Coursework'. Here, in Fig. 3.24, are examples of how some students presented their finished design.

It is important that you record any modifications you make to your original design during its manufacture.

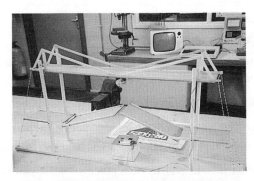
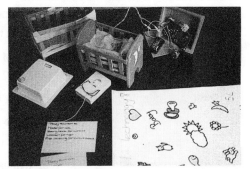

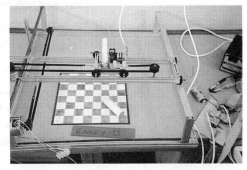
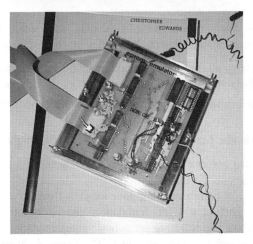

Fig. 3.24 Examples of how some students presented their final design

Remember. Making the developed idea is:

- When you use tools, manufacturing processes and a variety of materials to make your final idea.

7 > EVALUATING THE FINAL PRODUCT

66 Evaluation is a vital stage in the design process. 99

This is when you test and *evaluate* what you have made against the original criteria contained in your design brief and specification. It is important to see this part of the process in two stages:

Testing: using the product and producing information about its performance in relationship to the original *need*.

Evaluation: making judgements about the product in relationship to the original *design brief*.

Some of the mark schemes shown in the Examining Groups' syllabuses for coursework cover **both** of these aspects under *evaluation*. Others have a **separate** section for *testing* and another for *evaluation*. If you are to do well in this area it is important to cover both aspects in your work.

 **Some useful questions.**

At this stage it is useful to ask yourself, and others, the following questions about what you have made.

- Is it reliable and easy to use?
- Does it do the job outlined in the design brief?
- Is it safe to use?
- Is its appearance pleasing or functional?
- Can you think of any improvements?

Record any results from testing.

The results of testing and evaluation must be *recorded*. These results will provide you with information to improve the design. Remember, designs are seldom perfect the first time.

Remember. Evaluating the final product:

- Is about testing and then making judgements on the product's performance.
- Is about producing information which will help you to improve the design in the future.

In your evaluation it is helpful to take stock of what you *have* done. Ask yourself, and answer, questions such as:

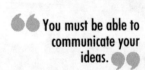 **Some useful questions about the process of designing**

- Where did I waste time?
- Could I improve on how I tackled the problem next time?
- Which part took longer than I planned?

The use of the design process offers you the opportunity to gain marks in all aspects of a CDT: Technology course if you a) **apply the process in a logical way using the stages which are appropriate to the task.** b) **always record and clearly communicate your ideas and decisions.**

8 COMMUNICATION SKILLS

Whatever it is you are designing it is only successful if you are able to properly *communicate* your ideas to others. You will want to be able to communicate your ideas to:

- your teachers so that they can understand what you are trying to do. This will help them to help you succeed and to mark your work properly.

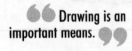 **You must be able to communicate your ideas.**

- the examiners who mark your work so that they can understand what you were trying to do.
- others (friends, parents, people in industry) who might help you in a variety of ways.

Whoever you are communicating your ideas to you must try to ensure that they clearly understand what you are doing.

The main way of communicating your ideas is through *drawing*.

Drawing is an important means.

If you took part in a CDT foundation course before starting your GCSE CDT: Technology course you will have some basic communication skills. You will also gain some further skills through the work in your CDT: Technology course. If you are also taking a course in CDT: Design and Communication you will have a further opportunity to practise and gain new communication skills.

This part of the book will not actually teach you these skills but it will show you some of the variety of skills you need to use and practise. You should gain these skills through the course you are taking at school.

Remember to communicate your ideas well.

- Think about what you want to say before you start.
- Choose the method of communication which will most clearly show what you want.
- Use the correct materials (paper, pencils, pens, colours – paint, crayons, felt tips) and always draw on a good surface.
- Practise the various ways of drawing – use those which you are most successful at. With practice, everyone can draw their ideas.

DRAWING

Fig. 3.25 presents some of the types of drawing you will need to use in various parts of the assessment.

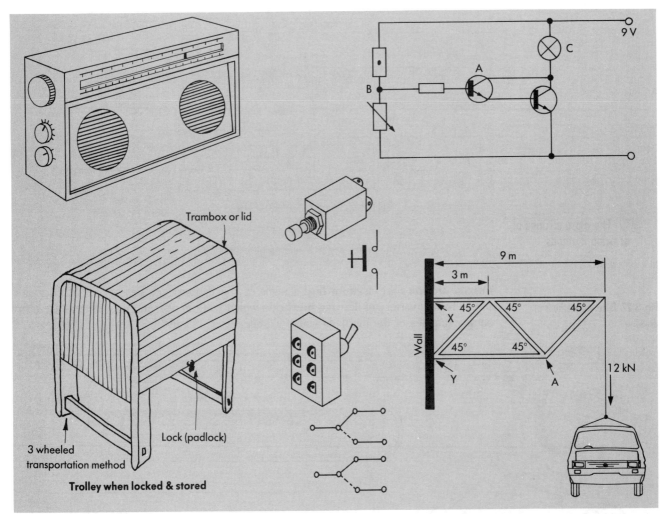

Fig. 3.25 Various types of drawing

Sketching is widely used. Usually you draw your ideas by using freehand sketches or formal drawings. *Freehand sketches*, as in Fig. 3.26, are the quick way of recording your ideas.

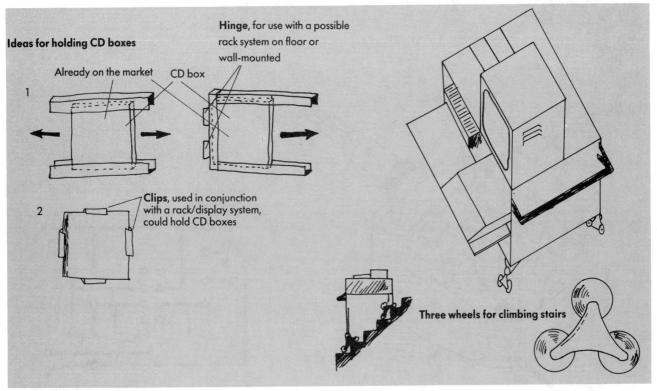

Fig. 3.26 Some freehand sketches

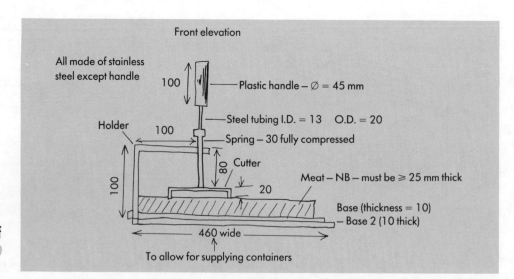

Front elevation

All made of stainless
steel except handle

100 — Plastic handle – ∅ = 45 mm

Holder

100 — Steel tubing I.D. = 13   O.D. = 20

— Spring – 30 fully compressed

Cutter

100

80

Meat – NB – must be ≥ 25 mm thick

20

Base (thickness = 10)
— Base 2 (10 thick)

460 wide

To allow for supplying containers

Formal drawings are used for final designs or special purposes such as circuit diagrams.
You have a variety of drawing **methods** which you can use. In Fig. 3.27 you are given
some examples of the methods you could use.

**Fig. 3.27 Different methods of
drawing**

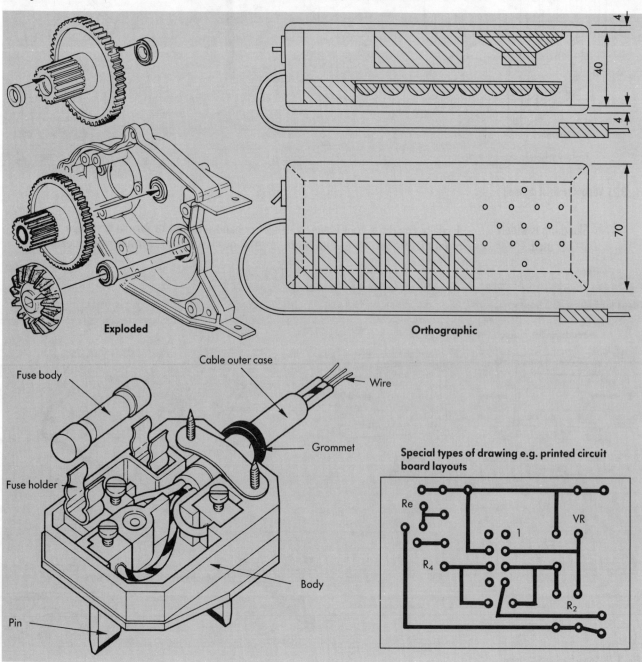

Exploded

Orthographic

40

70

4

4

Fuse body

Cable outer case

Wire

Grommet

Fuse holder

Body

Pin

**Special types of drawing e.g. printed circuit
board layouts**

Re

VR

1

R₄

R₂

❝ Shading and colour are important. ❞

It is also useful to use **colour** and **shading**. This can be used to make important parts of your drawings stand out or to highlight particular pieces of information. In the examples in Fig. 3.28 you can see different ways of using shading.

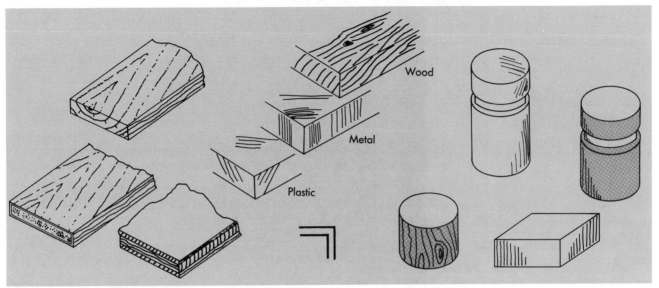

Fig. 3.28 Different ways of using shading

NOTES AND ANNOTATION

❝ Use notes with your drawing. ❞

As well as using sketches you will need to add *notes* to make your designs fully understood. It is better to use some of the methods shown below (Fig. 3.29) rather than writing as you would in an exercise book. The examples show how you can make your printing and your notes stand out.

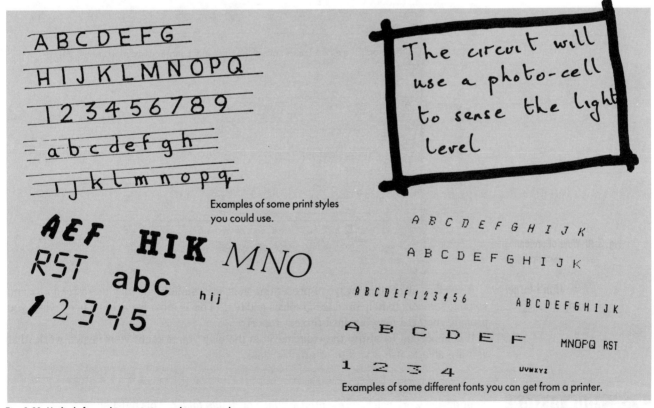

Fig. 3.29 Methods for making printing and notes stand out

STATISTICAL DATA

❝ Graphs and tables can help make things clear. ❞

Often in CDT:Technology you have to make use of *statistical data* as part of your design information. It is very useful to be able to present this in *graphical form*. In the examples in Fig. 3.30 you are shown some of the methods which you could use.

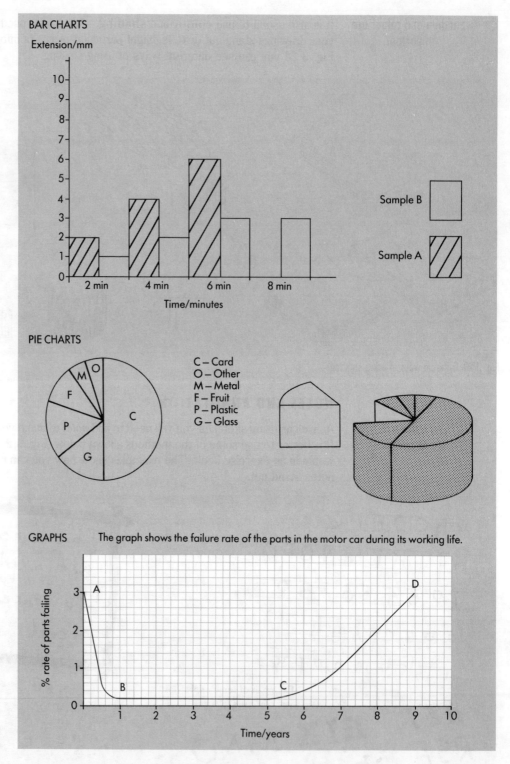

Fig. 3.30 Ways of presenting
statistical data

**❝❝ Don't forget
computers. ❞❞**

As well as all of these ways of presenting your information you may use a *computer* and
suitable *software* to help produce graphics and text. This is most likely to be used when you
prepare material for your final project report

It is important to **show** the examiners, in the way you present your design work, that
you are able to use a **range** of graphic skills.

Your design work will be presented in a *folio* or *design folder*. This must show:

**❝❝ Elements in your design
folio. ❞❞**

- How you identified the need from a situation or context.
- The design brief to which you worked.
- How you analysed the problems.
- The alternative ideas you began to develop.
- Models of some of your ideas.

- Why you decided upon the final idea you were going to develop.
- A series of working drawings and material specification for your final idea.
- Details of manufacture and any modifications you made.
- How you tested the finished product.
- The evaluation of the finished product against your original design criteria.

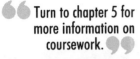
Turn to chapter 5 for more information on coursework.

In the example shown in Fig. 3.31 you can see how one student has developed his work to fit some of the stages given above.

We look more carefully at how to build up a folio in chapter 5.

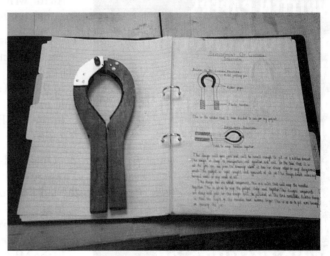

Fig. 3.31 Montage of student work

A FINAL STATEMENT

- The use of a range of graphic skills is how you communicate your ideas to others.
- Practise using a variety of skills.
- Think clearly about what you want to draw and say.
- Always ask yourself, 'Does this help to explain my ideas?'

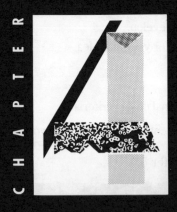

THE WRITTEN EXAMINATION

HOW THE WRITTEN PAPERS WORK

BASIC TECHNIQUES FOR WRITTEN PAPERS

QUESTIONS INVOLVING SKETCHING

QUESTIONS INVOLVING PLOTTING A GRAPH

DEALING WITH CALCULATIONS

NOTATION

BEING EXAMINED ON THE COMMON CORE

BEING EXAMINED ON THE OPTIONAL MODULES

GETTING STARTED

All the examining groups make use of written papers as part of their CDT: Technology syllabuses. If the examining group uses a *design examination* as part of the assessment then the *written papers* cover 30% of the final mark. If **no** design examination is used, then the *written papers* cover 50% of the final mark (except for NISEAC). Because of this difference in the contribution of the written papers to your final mark, it is important to find out which syllabus you are taking, when you start your course.

All the written examinations, with the exception of the NEAB syllabus A, consist of two parts.

1 A Common Core paper

In the SEG and WJEC syllabuses this paper will form 20% of your final mark.

In the MEG and ULEAC syllabuses this paper will form 10% of your final mark.

In the NISEAC syllabus this paper will form 30% of your final mark (Grade C–G) or 20% (Grade A–C).

2 Optional Module papers

These are the papers for the two optional modules which you choose at the start of your course.

In the SEG and WJEC syllabuses these papers will form 30% of your final mark; 15% for each module, unless you are taking one of the SEG *double modules* which will count for 30% of your final mark.

In the MEG and ULEAC syllabuses these papers will form 20% of your final mark; 10% for each module.

In the NISEAC syllabus this paper will form 25% of your final mark (Grade C–G). However if you take papers 2 and 3 (Grade A–C), then the optional modules will form 35% of your final mark.

For the NEAB syllabus A you do not have a Core and Module structure. However, you will sit two papers which will be based on the full subject content of the syllabus.

Paper 1 – will have a series of structured questions and form 25% of your final mark.

Paper 2 – will have a series of longer questions which will require complete solutions to a range of technological problems. This will also form 25% of your final mark.

ESSENTIAL PRINCIPLES

All of the written papers are sat under formal examination conditions and your answer papers are sent away to an examiner for marking.

In this chapter we will look at the following:

1 How the written papers work.
2 Basic techniques.
3 Dealing with calculations.
4 Notation.
1–4 are applicable to both the *Common Core* **and** the *Optional Modules* or, if you are taking NEA syllabus A, **both** *Papers 1* and *2*.
5 The Common Core.
6 The Optional Modules.

This chapter will not look at the detailed content of the Common Core and the Optional Modules; it is not the purpose of this book to replace the text book and the notes you will be using at school. However, it will show you how to prepare for the written examinations and to do the best you can in them.

Further detail on the subject content of your course can be gained from a variety of books, many of which may be in your school or the CDT department's library.

Some useful books to look at are:

■ *SCDC – Modular Courses in Technology.* There are books covering almost all of the Optional Modules.

■ *Take off with GCSE Technology.*

■ *Control Technology* – for SEG double module in Control Technology.

These will help to provide, with this book, a good background for your revision and preparation in GCSE CDT: Technology.

<table>
<tr><td>

1▷ HOW THE WRITTEN PAPERS WORK

❝ Check the subject content. ❞

❝ You are tested on knowledge, skills and application. ❞

</td><td>

The *written papers* are designed to test your knowledge and understanding of the subject content contained within the syllabus. At an early stage in your GCSE CDT: Technology course it is a good idea to look at the syllabus for the examination you are taking. In it you will find a list of **subject content** as in Fig. 4.3 below.

These are the aspects of *knowledge* which the written papers may test you on. Ask your teacher for a copy of your syllabus or write to your exam group (see page 6). You can then tick off each aspect as you cover it in your course. You can also make a note when you are sure that you know and understand a particular fact.

The written papers may also test your *design skills* and *communication skills*. The questions will be designed to test your understanding and *application* of knowledge rather than asking you to recall pure facts. An example is given below.

In Fig. 4.1 you are shown the circuit diagram and pictorial view of a variable kitchen timer.

</td></tr>
</table>

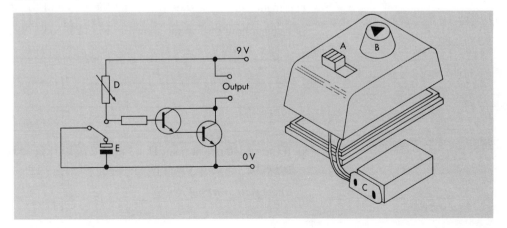

Fig. 4.1

Clearly indicate on the circuit diagram which parts are attached to the items marked **A, B** and **C** on the pictorial view.

(6)

Examiner comment

Here you are being asked to relate the circuit diagram to the controls of the product. The question is expecting you to show real understanding of the circuit and what parts are represented by the controls A, B and the battery connections C.

All of the papers are designed by the Chief Examiners to help you present your knowledge and thinking as clearly as possible. In the examination you will be given **either** an answer booklet with questions, diagrams, photographs and clearly marked spaces for your answers, for example see Fig. 4.2 below, **or** a question paper with a writing booklet attached.

LEAG also use a *theme* throughout all of the papers to help you. You must be prepared to write, do simple calculations, sketch, draw diagrams and graphs, as part of your answers.

Look at past papers.

Well before you sit the examination look at some past papers to familiarise yourself with the style used by the Examining Group whose course you are taking. Apart from the differences in instructions and presentation of the papers, two different approaches are used by the Examining Group for the *Common Core* and *Module* papers.

1   Some groups have a paper where you are asked to attempt **all** questions.
2   Others have a paper where you have a **section A** with a series of shorter questions and a **section B** with two longer questions, from which you **choose one**.

Some groups use style 1 for the Common Core and style 2 for the Optional Modules.

However, no matter which style is used the papers are designed to have an incline of difficulty. This means that the stages of a question should become progressively harder.

In Fig. 4.2 you are shown the circuit diagram and pictorial view of a variable kitchen timer.

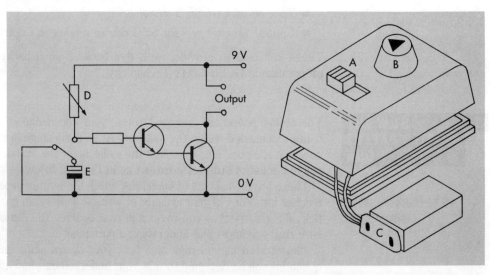

Fig. 4.2

a)   Clearly indicate on the circuit diagram which parts are attached to the items marked **A, B** and **C** on the pictorial view.   (6)

b)   The manufacturer wishes to extend the range of the timer.

i) Explain how the circuit shown in Fig. 4.2 could be modified to do this.

_____

_____

_____

_____   (4)

ii) If the resistance at point **D** in Fig. 4.2 is $100\,k\Omega$ and a $1000\,\mu F$ capacitor is fitted at point **E**, calculate the time constant for the capacitor.

Show your working here.

Time constant = _____   (4)

Examiner comment

Each stage of this question is testing different skills and knowledge and is becoming harder for most candidates at each stage.

Part a) needs a basic practical understanding of the circuit.

Part b) i) requires some real knowledge of how the circuit works.

Part b) ii) requires this knowledge and the ability to perform a calculation.

The fact that the question has parts which get harder may mean that you find there are parts of a question which you cannot do. Do not worry; attempt all of the parts you can. Also always **look completely through** a question and indeed completely through the whole paper; getting an 'incline of difficulty' correct is very difficult even for the Chief Examiner and there may be parts you **can** do, further on in the question or paper.

A FINAL STATEMENT

- The written papers will test the subject content of the syllabus.
- Make sure you know what it is you may be tested on. Look at the syllabus subject content to see what you have to know.
- Look at past question papers.

2 >	BASIC TECHNIQUES FOR WRITTEN PAPERS

> Draw up your own check list.

In this section we will look at some basic techniques to help ensure that you are able to do your best in the written papers.

- When you look at the subject content of the syllabus for your course you may wonder how you will ever know everything that is there. Do not worry; by the time you sit your examination much of this content you will **know**, and will be happily **using**, through your project and design work. What remains is what you will need to revise and practise, well before your examination.

It will help to have a copy of your syllabus content and to make a simple check sheet, like the one in Fig. 4.3.

G.C.S.E. EXAMINATIONS JUNE 1991			I have covered	I know this	I need to revise	I need to practise
	2.4	demonstrate a competence in the safe and proper use and maintenance of tools, equipment and machines.				
3 Communication	3.1	demonstrate a competence in a range of communication skills including written, number and graphical and the use of appropriate symbols;	✓	✓		✓
	3.2	demonstrate a competence in the use of a technical and scientific vocabulary;				
	3.3	demonstrate a competence in the use of symbolic notation of the contents of the common core.	✓		✓	✓
Knowledge 4 Material Resources	4.1	classify materials into types e.g. wood, metal, plastics, ceramics/mixtures;	✓	✓		
	4.2	describe the sources of common materials and distinguish between those that occur naturally and those that have been processed;	✓	✓		
	4.3	give examples of the use of alloying, laminating and mixing materials to improve properties of strength, hardness and resistance to corrosion.	✓		✓	
	4.4	select for a given application, the most suitable material based on cost, availability, strength/weight ratio, mechanical, electrical and physical properties, corrosion resistance and environmental considerations.				
5 Energy	5.1	describe the main energy resources available to man, i.e. coal, oil, gas, wind, water, the sun and nuclear energy;	✓	✓		

G.C.S.E. EXAMINATIONS JUNE 1991

		I have covered	I know this	I need to revise	I need to practise
	5.2 list the following forms of energy and give examples of devices which will change one form into another – mechanical, electrical, chemical, heat, light and sound;	✓			✓
	5.3 use the relationship between work done, force and distance moved; perform calculations based on this relationship;	✓		✓	
	5.4 define the efficiency of an energy system in terms of work input and output;	✓	✓		
	5.5 recognise society's dependence on energy and describe measures to conserve energy in transport, industry and the home.	✓	✓		
6 Control	6.1 describe electric current as a flow of charge normally carried by electrons;	✓	✓		
	6.2 use and describe applications of switches in simple circuits;	✓		✓	
	6.3 use and describe applications of an interface device using an electromagnetic relay as an example;				
	6.4 use and describe applications of the following output devices – electric motor, electromagnetic solenoid and counter, bell, buzzer, filament bulb;	✓		✓	
	6.5 design and build simple control circuits using the above components;				
	6.6 use and describe the operation of levers, linkages, pulleys and belts, chains, gears, cams, eccentrics, pawls and ratchets in simple mechanical systems;	✓	✓		✓
	6.7 describe and give examples of the following types of motion – linear, rotary, reciprocating and oscillating;	✓	✓		✓

Fig. 4.3 A check sheet for revision and practice

- Also, remember that there will often be too much content in a syllabus for the Chief Examiner to be able to set a question on **everything**. Look at the past papers to see if certain aspects occur each year. Your teacher may give you a list of the main areas of content to revise.

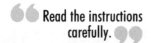 **Read the instructions carefully.**

- Well before you take the written examination familiarise yourself with the **style** of the papers. Pay particular attention to the instructions on the **front cover** (Fig. 4.4).

MIDLAND EXAMINING GROUP   **1451/6**
General Certificate of Secondary Education

CDT – TECHNOLOGY
PAPER 6   STRUCTURES MODULE   40 minutes

This paper will be taken with Paper 2 and that for the other module stated in your entry. All three papers are to be taken together in one session of 2 hours.

Additional materials provided by the Board:
1. Additional answer paper, if required.
Instructions to candidates:
Answer **one** *question.*

Sketch diagrams should be given where appropriate.

The intended marks for parts of questions are given in brackets [ ].

Answer the question selected on the attached answer sheet provided for this module.

Write your name, centre and candidate numbers in the spaces provided on the front of the answer sheet.

At the end of the examination detach the answer sheet, attach any additional paper used, and hand it to the Supervisor for despatch to the examiner for this paper.

Fig. 4.4 Take note of the instructions on the front cover of your exam paper

Look at the front cover of the papers for **your** syllabus. Each exam group has a different style for presenting its instructions.

Answer the right number of questions.

- The instructions will tell you what to do, how many questions to answer etc. Often candidates lose marks by **not** following the instructions or by answering all of the questions, when they only have to answer one. This will also lose you time and may mean that you do not do as well as you could.

Read through all the questions.

- When you are **in** the examination room, read the instructions on the front of the paper carefully, then read through the whole paper. Do not rush into answering questions; you have more time than you think. Also check that the titles of the optional modules are the same as the ones your teacher has said you were taking.

Ask, if you're worried.

- If there is anything which seems wrong, or the optional modules are different from the ones you thought you were taking, ask the **invigilator** (the person supervising the exam) before you start. The examination system is very complicated and sometimes mistakes do happen.

Make sure you are answering the question actually set.

- When you **open** the papers, look carefully at the questions. Read each question before you attempt it: make sure you understand what is asked and keep checking as you write that you are answering the question. The example (Fig. 4.5) shows how a candidate has **failed** to answer the question.

(a) Select a suitable material for each of the uses in the table below.
Toughened glass   Plastic laminate   Polythene   Nylon   Copper
PTFE   Beech   Stainless Steel   Brass   Ceramic

USE	MATERIAL
Kitchen worktop surface	PLASTIC LAMINATE
Food processor cutting blades	STAINLESS STEEL
Insert for the base of a saucepan	COPPER
See-through oven door	TOUGHENED GLASS
Non-stick surface of frying pans	PTFE
Freezer containers	POLYTHENE

(b) For each of the following uses give one specific property of the material you have chosen, which makes it suitable for the given use.

(i) Insert for the base of a saucepan.

   Copper is good it is strong, it lasts long.

(ii) Freezer containers.

   Plastic is good as it is clear, you can see food.

_____ *(4)*

Fig. 4.5 Student answer to question

Examiner comment

This candidate has answered part a) of the question correctly. However, part b) is very general and has not answered the question. The examiner is looking for one key property which makes the material suitable for use e.g.

b) i) Copper is a good conductor.

   ii) Plastic does not become brittle at low temperatures.

- If a **list is provided**, use it. Look back to Fig. 4.5, part (a). If you are asked to select from the list, then don't add in answers that are **not** on that list.

- If the papers for your course are of the type where you answer in the space provided, make sure you **use** the space. If you find you need **more than** the space provided, you are probably saying more than is required to earn the marks.

- Give answers in full. For example, if you are asked:

What is the meaning of the term *rpm*?

   Revs per min

The **full** answer should be given, i.e. 'revolutions per minute'.

- Always make your answers clear and concise. If the question asks for a *sketch* or *diagram* then use one in your answer; there will be marks for it. Often candidates lose marks by **not** sketching or using diagrams when asked.

    If sketches are asked for, provide a simple, clear sketch as an answer, labelled appropriately. Fig. 4.6 is an appropriate answer to the question: **sketch a suitable drive mechanism for a food processor.**

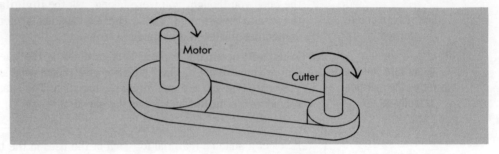

Fig. 4.6 Simple, clear sketch

In Fig. 4.7 you are shown a stainless steel sink and a polythene washing-up bowl. Both of these articles are formed from sheet materials.

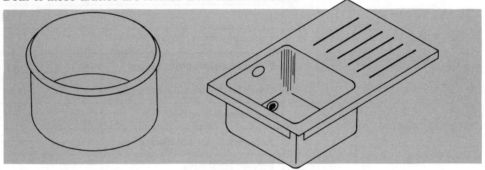

Fig. 4.7

With notes and sketches explain how either the sink or the washing-up bowl are formed.

   The sink is made by press forming. I think you use the following stages.

   1) Sheet stainless steel placed in press

   2) Press operated - sheet is pushed into shape over mould.

   This will form the basic shape.

Examiner comment

This answer has a simple sequence in the correct order but has given very little detailed information. Also sketches are clearly asked for in the question. It is, then, most important that they are given as part of the answer.

- If you have been asked to *plot a graph*, check that you have put the points in the **correct places**. Have you *labelled* the curve(s) and the axis? Have you chosen appropriate *units* for each axis? Have you chosen sensible *divisions* for the units on each axis? (look at Fig. 4.9 – units of 10°C would have provided more information than the units of 20°C actually used for temperature on the vertical axis).

As part of a consumer test two electric kettles are filled with water and then boiled. One has a plastic body and one has a stainless steel body. In the bar graph, Fig. 4.8 you are shown how the temperature of the water, in each kettle, falls over a period of time.

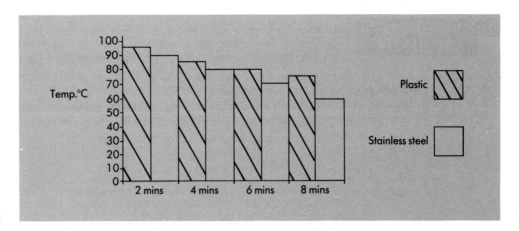

Fig. 4.8

a) Plot a cooling curve for each kettle. Clearly label each curve. (10)

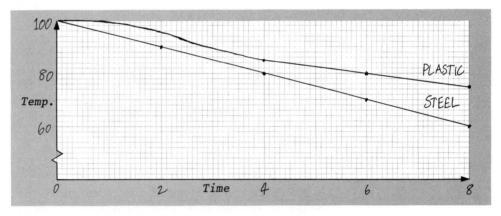

Fig. 4.9

b) From the information, state which kettle is better at keeping the water warm and give **one** reason why.

> Both kettles seem good at keeping warm. After eight minutes I think both would still have a high enough temperature allow you to make a cup of tea. The steel kettle is a little bit cooler but I do not think it would make any difference. (3)

Examiner comment

The curves in the graph (Fig. 4.9) are labelled and broadly correct. There is a 'rogue' point at Time 6 minutes. The temperature scale could have had divisions of 10°C rather than 20°C to help the reader interpret the graph.

The candidate has failed to answer part b) of the question. The answer is very general and does not give what the examiner has asked. Again a very simple response is needed e.g.

The plastic kettle is better at keeping the water warm. This is because it is a good insulator.

Even the following response is sufficient:

Plastic; it is a good insulator.

Both of these responses easily fit the space provided.

Remember for 3 marks you will need a fairly simple, concise answer only.

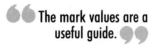

- Look at the mark values which are printed by the side of each question or part of a question. These give a guide as to how much detail you are expected to provide.

- Do not get stuck on a question or part of a question with a low mark value if there is something else with a high mark value you can still do. When you first read through the paper it is helpful to **tick** the questions you know you can answer.

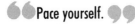

- During the examination, keep a check on the time so that you do not run out of time before you have attempted the questions you can do best.

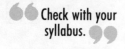

5 DEALING WITH CALCULATIONS

❝ Check with your syllabus. ❞

In any GCSE CDT: Technology written examination, you will almost certainly be asked to perform a calculation, plot a graph or carry out some similar mathematical based task. Usually this will only be part of a question, sometimes the information you have gained by performing the calculation or by plotting the graph will be used in the next part of the question. For example:

i) Different masses are attached to the dough-hook in order to vary the resistance to the motion. In the example above the resistance to the motion is 2 N. What is the work done in **one** revolution of the dough-hook?

Work done = _____

_____

_____ units _____ (3)

ii) What is the power being used in turning the dough-hook?

Power = _____

_____

_____ units _____ (3)

The calculations will be based on the formulae and equations which are given in the subject content of your syllabus. By the time you sit the examination you will be very familiar with some, whilst others will be far less familiar. To help you, some of the examination groups give you the formulae and equations which are used in the question paper at the beginning, such as in the NEA example, below.

Candidates should use, where appropriate, the formulae given below when answering questions which include calculations.

1. Work done = force × distance moved in the direction of the force ($W = f \times d$)

2. Kinetic Energy = ½ × mass × (velocity)^2 ($KE = \frac{1}{2} \times m \times v^2$)

3. Potential Energy = mass × gravitational field strength × height ($PE = mgh$)

4. Energy = potential difference × current × time ($E = VIt$)

5. Power = $\dfrac{\text{work done}}{\text{time taken}}$

6. Electrical Power = current × potential difference

7. Efficiency = $\dfrac{\text{work output}}{\text{work input}} \times 100\%$

   or = $\dfrac{\text{energy output}}{\text{energy input}} \times 100\%$

8. Potential Difference = current × resistance ($V = IR$)

9. For potential divider $V_1 = \dfrac{R_1}{(R_1 + R_2)} \times V$

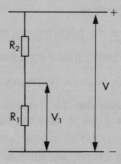

Fig. 4.10

10. Series Resistors $R_{TOTAL} = R_1 + R_2 + R_3$ etc.

    Parallel Resistors $\dfrac{1}{R_{TOTAL}} = \dfrac{1}{R_1} + \dfrac{1}{R_2} + \dfrac{1}{R_3}$ etc.

11 Series batteries $V_{TOTAL} = V_1 + V_2 + V_3$

12 Moment of a force $=$ force $\times$ perpendicular distance from pivot

13 For equilibrium
        Sum of clockwise moments $=$ Sum of anticlockwise moments
            Sum of coplanar forces $=$ zero

14 Gear ratio of a simple gear train $= \dfrac{\text{number of teeth on driver gear}}{\text{number of teeth on driven gear}}$

(N.B. For a compound gear train

        Total Gear ratio $=$ the product of the gear ratios of all the sub-systems
            i.e. $G.R_T = G.R_1 \times G.R_2 \times G.R_3 \ldots$ etc.)

                                                                                    (NEAB)

Other exam groups will give you the less familiar formulae or equations as part of the question, *where they are being used* (i.e. not at the beginning of the paper).

In Fig. 4.11 you are shown a circuit which will produce a series of regular pulses as an output at pin 3 of the IC.

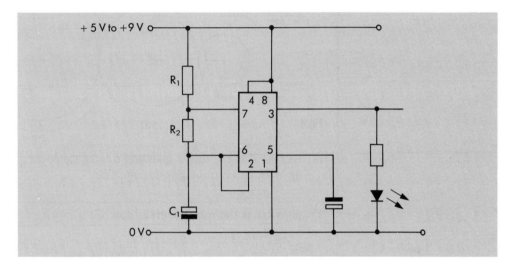

Fig. 4.11

Given that the values of components $R_1 = 100\,k\Omega$, $R_2 = 50\,k\Omega$, $C_1 = 10\,\mu F$ in Fig. 4.11

i) Calculate the time the indicator LED will be on.
   Use the equation
      $t = (R_1 + R_2)\,C_1$ where $t_1 =$ time in seconds, R $=$ ohms, C $=$ farads.

      Time LED on ————————   (6)

ii) Calculate the time the indicator LED will be off.
    Use the equation
      $t = R_2 C_1$ where $t =$ time in seconds, R $=$ ohms, C $=$ farads

      Time LED off ————————   (6)
                                                                              (ULEAC)

Some groups will expect you to be able to remember them. Check to make sure you know what is the case in **your** exam.

In the *Common Core* paper the calculations may well be fairly simple and of a general nature. In the *Optional Modules* they will be specific to the content of the module and may be quite complicated with several stages to them.

  Sometimes, as in the previous question, there will be a space provided for the calculation. Sometimes there will be a specially provided space for your *working*, as well as for your *answer*.

66 Remember to write
down the units. **99**

66 Show the method you
have used. **99**

When you answer a calculation question it is often very easy just to write down the answer. This is particularly so if you have done all of the work on a calculator. If you do this, make sure that you give the appropriate *units* for your answer. Often there is one mark for expressing your answer in the appropriate units.

While you can earn full marks for only giving the answer with the correct units, it is a dangerous thing to do. If you have made any mistake you can lose all of the marks for the calculation because the examiner cannot see **how** you arrived at the answer and where you went wrong. It is much better to show your working in clear stages, even if you do use a calculator.

Usually the *marks* for any calculation question are broken down into *stages* so that the examiner can give you credit up to the point where you go wrong. Fig. 4.12 shows such a question.

In Fig. 1 you are shown a simple gear train which is part of the drive mechanism in a child's toy.

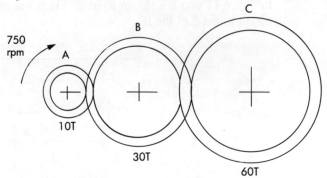

Fig. 1

(a) As gear *A* is the driver gear and rotates clockwise.
    (i) What is the name given to gear *B*?

        IDLER

    (ii) What is the name given to gear *C*?

        DRIVEN

    (iii) What is the direction of rotation of gear *C*?

        CLOCKWISE   *(3)*

(b) Using the information given in Fig. 1 calculate the gear ratio and output (rotational) velocity of the system.

Show your working here.

$$VR = \frac{10}{60} = \frac{1}{6} = 6:1$$

66 Use of:
number of teeth on driven
number of teeth on driver
Answer expressed as a ratio. **99**

Rotary velocity

$$\frac{750 \times 10}{60} = \frac{750}{6}$$

66 Use of:
rotary velocity of driver × teeth on driver
      number of teeth on driven. **99**

$$\frac{750}{6} = 125 \, r.p.m.$$

Gear ratio =   6:1

Output (rotational) velocity of system =   125 r.p.m.   *(6)*

Examiner comment

Clear stages for each part of the calculation are shown. Note that in this situation the idler gear is not used in the calculation.

Fig. 4.12 Show the stages in your calculation

> **Question 2**
>
> If the base current I_b of Tr_1 changes through the range 0.01 mA to 0.06 mA and the collector current I_c changes through range 8 mA to 26 mA, calculate the gain of the transistor.
>
> Show your working here.
>
> $$\frac{26 - 8mA}{0.06 - 0.01mA} =$$
>
> $$\frac{18}{0.05} = 360$$
>
> " Correct use of:
> change in collect current
> change in base current.
> Correct transposition of data from question. "
>
> Gain of transistor = $\underline{\quad 360 \quad}$ _____ (3)

Examiner comment

The working has been set out in clear stages showing how the answer is obtained. If any stage was wrong, the examiner could see where the mistake was made and give credit up to that point.

If the examiner **cannot see** the stages in your calculation, you cannot be given credit. Also there are often marks in a calculation question for translating the information from the question into the calculation and where necessary for transposing the formulae or equation. Again if the examiner **cannot see** this in your working, you cannot be given the credit.

Remember. You can deal with a calculation more easily:

- if you show the stages of your working,
- if you remember the basic equations or formulae to use,
- if you use a calculator to help you,
- if you practise the calculations you use regularly.

Calculations will form part of your written examination. Check to see if the syllabus you are taking gives the formulae or equations needed in the examination paper.

Do not worry if your mathematics is not very good. If you go through the calculation stage by stage it will help. Remember, the calculation is only one **part** of the question or paper.

6 ⟩ NOTATION

" Become familiar with technical notation. "

In all of the written papers and in other parts of your CDT: Technology course, you will have to interpret and draw diagrams. These are often given in the form of a *technical notation*. This means that certain symbols are used to convey the information: perhaps the most familiar example is a circuit diagram (Fig. 4.13).

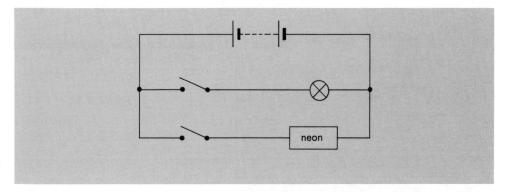

Fig. 4.13 Simple parallel circuit design

Some of the notation used will be specific to the *Optional Modules* you will be taking and is covered later in the Optional Modules section. However, the following examples are more general and will often be used in the Common Core paper.

Fig. 4.14 presents some of the symbols and diagram presentations you will see in the *Common Core* paper.

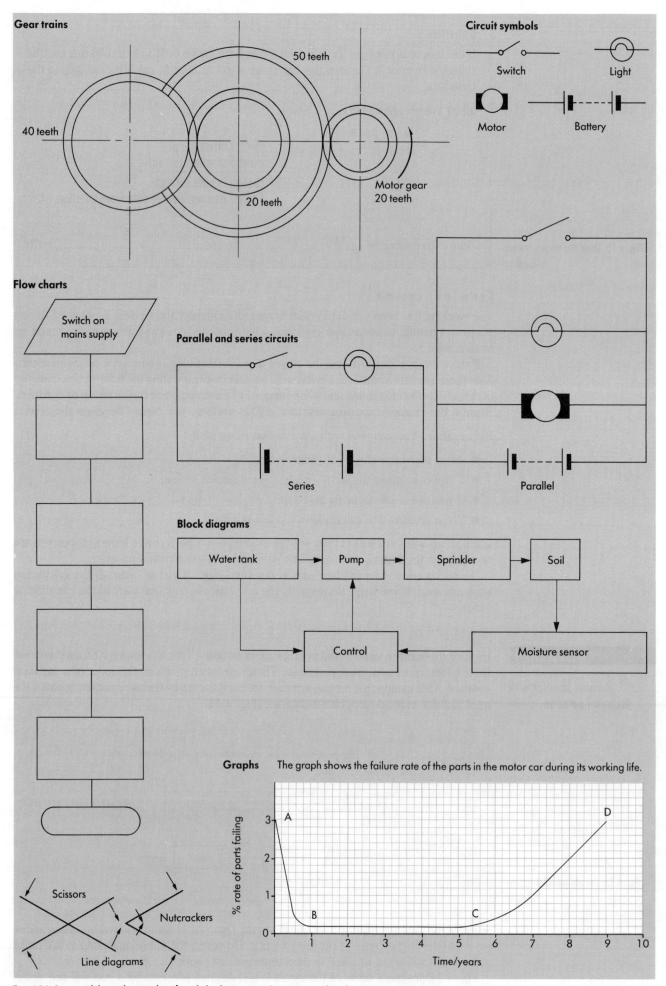

Gear trains

40 teeth

50 teeth

20 teeth

Motor gear
20 teeth

Circuit symbols

Switch   Light

Motor   Battery

Flow charts

Switch on
mains supply

Parallel and series circuits

Series   Parallel

Block diagrams

Water tank → Pump → Sprinkler → Soil

Control ← Moisture sensor

Graphs   The graph shows the failure rate of the parts in the motor car during its working life.

% rate of parts failing

A   D

B   C

Time/years

Scissors

Nutcrackers

Line diagrams

Fig. 4.14 Some widely used examples of symbols, diagrams and notation used in the Common Core paper

It is important that you become familiar with understanding and using this range of notation. Without this familiarity you will find it difficult to understand or answer many of the questions in both the Common Core and Optional module papers.

As with the subject content of the syllabus, much of the notation will become familiar by use. For example, if you are studying the electronics module and also do an electronics based project then you will almost certainly gain a full understanding of circuit diagrams and circuit symbols. You may need to revise some of the notation for line diagrams or mechanical systems which may be used in the Common Core paper.

So much of what you will need to revise here will certainly depend upon the particular modules and course you are taking.

A FINAL STATEMENT

- Notation is a type of shorthand for diagrams and symbols.
- Notation is used throughout a CDT: Technology course.
- As with the subject content you will need to revise well in advance of the examination.
- Some aspects will become familiar from use, others you will need to practise.

In preparation for the written examination you will have a set of technology notes and possibly a text book from which to revise. Use your content check list to see which areas you need to concentrate your revision on. Your teacher may give you a revision list or, towards the end of the course, set revision topics on which to answer past questions. Try answering past questions and complete papers. At first do this with no time limit, trying to get everything right; then set yourself the same time as in the examination and see how much you can now do.

Remember. The written examination will be easier if you:

- Make sure you understand your work. If there is anything you do not understand find out as soon as possible.
- Revise your work in stages throughout the course.
- Try to reach the point where some of the basic principles you regularly use do not have to be revised.
- Test yourself to see how much you can remember. It helps to do this as a group.
- Make a clear plan for your final revision. Start about 12 weeks before the written examination.
- Look at past papers. Practise answering questions, sometimes setting yourself the same time limit that you will have in the exam.
- Use the night before the examination to relax. Do something which is not connected with CDT: Technology.

7 > BEING EXAMINED ON THE COMMON CORE

The Common Core is a vital part of your course.

The *Common Core* is an integral part of all CDT: Technology syllabuses and underpins, with the *design process*, the work you do in the whole course. This statement by one of the exam groups will give you an idea of the importance of the common core.

COMMON CORE

In the teaching of Technology it has often been forgotten that there is a commonality in Technology between all its discrete areas. This syllabus has sought to redress that, and in consequence it will be seen that the questions in the 'live' examination will be wider ranging than the questions in the specimen paper.

The design and problem solving area has been well covered both in this booklet and in the examination format and centres will be well advised to look again at the full width of the core, both in terms of skills and knowledge.

There will be an expectation that candidates will be able to comment about their experiences of technology in their lives, both as consumers and as practitioners. Visits to various industrial applications and reading around the subject should encourage a breadth of thought that could well be focused at an awareness level within the examination.

GCSE is about understanding, not just knowledge and, as previously mentioned, questions will be set on the full range of the common core, which will encourage pupils to demonstrate their understanding. Completion charts, sequence diagrams, interpretation of graphical data are just some of the areas that pupils could be usefully encouraged to have seen.

The knowledge area of the common core should be seen to pervade all the activity in CDT: Technology; it is a tool kit that pupils should be encouraged to develop and utilise. Technology is using knowledge, making judgements and in all things seeking to understand and balance both the advantages and disadvantages of technological change.

(ULEAC)

Whatever syllabus you are taking, the Common Core involves a range of design, making and communication skills as well as knowledge. You can expect to be tested on both the skills and knowledge in the Common Core paper. Much of this you will use regularly throughout your course. However, you should allow time to revise the knowledge part of the Common Core well in advance of the examination. Check the content of your own syllabus.

SAMPLE QUESTIONS

The following are example questions, with comments, taken from the various examining groups.

Question 1

This example shows how questions in the Common Core will often be set on everyday topics which are familiar and accessible to you.

Marks

a) Name the type of switch used to operate the interior light of a refrigerator.

_____ *(2)*

b) Is this a normally closed or normally open switch?

_____ *(2)*

c) With notes and sketches explain the operation of the refrigerator light.

(ULEAC example)

Question 2

These two questions are looking at computing as an aspect of the Common Core. However, there is an overall theme involving the relationship between Technology and Society within each question.

i) Computers are often used as a source of amusement, to play games on. In industry, they have other uses. Give **two** examples of the use of computers in industry.

a) _____

_____ *(1)*

b) _____

_____ *(1)*

ii) Briefly explain why a manufacturer might welcome the introduction of computers to a factory or office, but the workforce might not be so keen.

_____

_____

_____

_____

_____ *(3)*

(MEG examples)

Question 3

This example from SEG is looking at the areas of control, safety and electricity within the Common Core.

Fig. 4.15 shows part of a car's headlight circuit.

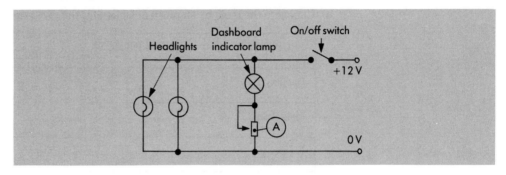

Fig. 4.15

a) State why the two headlamp bulbs are connected in parallel.

Answer: _____ *(1)*

b) i) Name component A.

Answer: _____ *(1)*

ii) State the purpose of component A in this circuit.

Answer: _____

_____ *(1)*

c) i) Name a safety device which can be included in the circuit to restrict the current to a safe maximum value.

Answer: _____

ii) Draw the symbol for this device.

iii) Mark on Fig. 4.15 with a cross where this device should be connected.   *(3)*

d) Complete Fig. 4.16 so that the component S switches on either the main or the dipped beam.   *(4)*

(SEG)

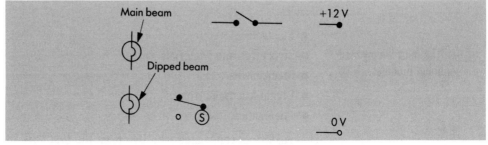

Fig. 4.16

Question 4

This question is looking at the candidate's understanding of materials and their properties.

a) Complete the table below by choosing, from the following list, the correct property for the definitions given:

hardness; plasticity; conductivity; toughness; strength.   (4)

PROPERTY	DEFINITION
	Deforms under load and does not return to its original shape when the load is removed.
	Resists abrasion and penetration.
	Withstands shock loads without fracture.
	Withstands loads which tend to make it increase in length.

b) Complete the table by stating a definition for the given property.   (4)

PROPERTY	DEFINITION
Ductility	
Malleability	
Elasticity	
Brittleness	

c) Explain what is meant by the term *thermal conductivity*.   (2)

_____

_____

(WJEC)

By the time of your examination you should be very familiar with using the skills and knowledge needed for the Common Core of your syllabus. You can expect to be examined on the *full range* of the Common Core's skills and knowledge.

8 ▶ BEING EXAMINED ON THE OPTIONAL MODULES

These are the papers based on the two *modules* of study you have followed in your course. They are called Optional modules because in each syllabus there is a wide range to choose from.

You can see from Table 1.1 that each Examining Group has a very similar list. The main differences are in the number of modules offered and in that some groups offer 'structures and materials' *together* whilst others offer them as *separate modules*. SEG have two very specialised double modules in control and microprocessor control.

However, the choice is usually made for you, by your school or teacher. Often the choice will be dependent upon the equipment your school has, or the range of experience possessed by your teachers. In fact most candidates take two from the following list of modules.

■ Electronics
■ Structures and Materials
■ Mechanisms
■ Digital Microelectronics
■ Pneumatics

66 The most widely used optional modules. 99

The majority of candidates take two from the *first three* in this list.

In the examination you will be tested upon the subject content of the modules you have studied. The questions will test your knowledge and understanding, and your ability to apply this to actual problems.

Remember, much of what you need to know you will have already acquired through the design and practical work which you have undertaken in your course. Also, remember that the optional modules are only a small element of your whole course.

If you follow the suggestions in the earlier part of the chapter and make use of your textbook and course notes you will be able to do your best in each module.

SAMPLE QUESTIONS

The following are example questions, with comments, on some of the widely used optional modules. This will give you an idea of the type of assessment you will face. If you attempt the ones on the modules relevant to you, you will be able to revise and practise the main knowledge areas that are likely to be assessed.

ELECTRONICS

Question 1 and outline answer

This question is asking you to show your understanding of the circuit through a systems approach.

In Fig. 4.17 you are shown part of the control circuit for the water temperature of a dishwasher.

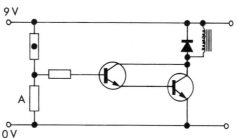

Fig. 4.17

Complete the block diagram for the circuit shown in Fig. 4.17. Clearly show the **input, process** and **output** stages of the circuit.   (8)

Fig. 4.18

Question 2 and outline answer

In Fig. 4.19 you are shown the circuit diagram and pictorial view of a variable kitchen timer.

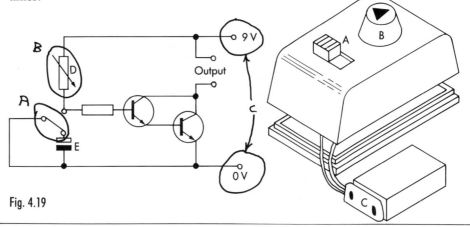

Fig. 4.19

a) Clearly indicate on the circuit diagram which parts are attached to the items marked **A**, **B** and **C** on the pictorial view. (6)

b) The manufacturer wishes to extend the range of the timer.

  i) Explain how the circuit shown in Fig. 4.19 could be modified to do this.

  Change values of variable resistor D and capacitor E.

  (4)

  ii) If the resistance at point **D** in Fig. 4.19 is 100 kΩ and a 1000 µF capacitor is fitted at point **E**, calculate the time constant for the capacitor.

  Show your working here. Use *T = C × R*

  100,000 × 0.001

  Time constant = *100 seconds* (4)

  iii) Explain the meaning of the term *time constant*.

  Time taken to change to $\frac{2}{3}$

  (2)

  iv) When a trial circuit is made, only one of each of the following capacitors is available:

  100 µF   200 µF   680 µF

  With a sketch show how you would arrange them to make a total capacitance of 1000 µF. (The example answer is shown in Fig. 4.20). (4)

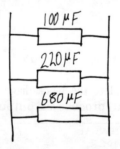

Fig. 4.20 Student answer to 2 b) iv)

c) In Fig. 4.21(b) you are shown a prototype PCB, which has been made for the timer.

  When this board is used the circuit fails because of faults in the PCB design. Clearly ring **two** faults you can see on the PCB in Fig. 4.21(b). (4)

  (ULEAC)

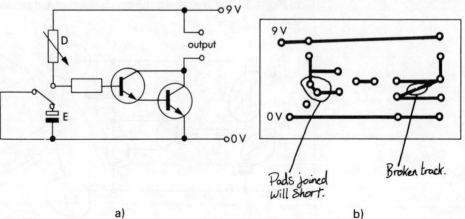

a)   b)

Fig. 4.21

Practice questions

1   The Table shows the colour code for resistors.

COLOUR	CODE
black	0
brown	1
red	2
orange	3
yellow	4
green	5
blue	6
violet	7
grey	8
white	9
tolerance	
gold	5%
silver	10%

a) State the value and tolerance of the resistor shown in Fig. 4.22.

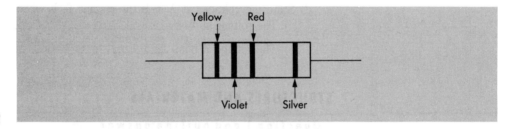

Fig. 4.22

    i) Value: _____ (1)

    ii) Tolerance: _____ (1)

b) A circuit requires a resistance of $6.9\,k\Omega$
What value of resistor should be connected in series with the resistor shown in Fig. 4.22 to achieve this?

    Value: _____ (1)

c) State the colour code which indicates this value.

    Colour Code (reading from left hand end)

_____   _____   _____

(2)
(SEG)

2   The two bulbs of the circuit in Fig. 4.23 are to flash so as to warn motorists of a hazard.

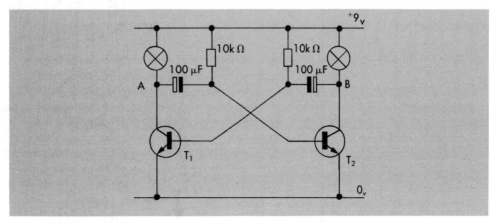

Fig. 4.23

    a) Name the circuit in Fig. 4.23

_____ (1)

b) When the circuit is built the bulbs flash too quickly.

   i) State **one** type of component that could be changed to make the bulbs flash at a slower rate.

_____

   ii) State a suitable value for the changed component that will halve the rate of flashing.

_____ (2)

c) Each bulb flashes for the same length of time. The waveform obtained on an oscilloscope is shown in Fig. 4.24.

Fig. 4.24

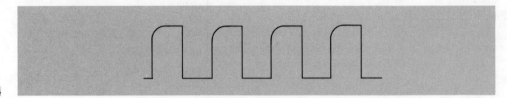

Label 'mark', 'space', and 'amplitude' on the diagram in Fig. 4.24. (3)

d) State the voltages at A & B the instant T_1 is ON and T_2 is OFF.
   i) The voltage at A is: _____
   ii) The voltage at B is: _____ (2)

                                                        (SEG)

STRUCTURES AND MATERIALS

Question 1 and outline answer

The drawing below (Fig. 4.25) shows a sectional view of a tap used by elderly persons.

The special handle is held in place by the pin which passes through the spindle.

To operate the tap the handle is moved in the direction shown and the threaded spindle closes the washer onto the body.

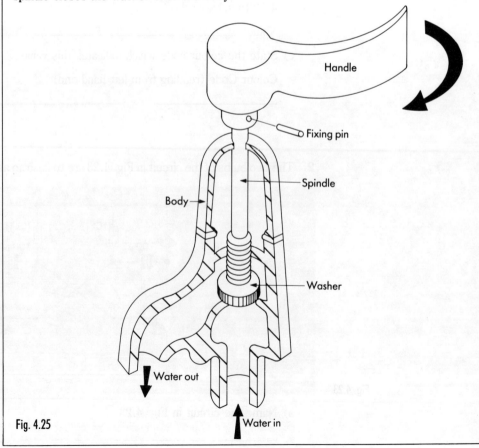

Fig. 4.25

a) Using the list, choose the word which best describes the forces acting in the following members:

tension   compression   shear   torsion   bending

i) The handle _BENDING_

ii) The pin _SHEAR_

iii) The spindle _TORSION_

iv) The washer _COMPRESSION_ (4)

b) The material which is commonly used for taps is brass. It is an alloy of **two** metals.

i) What are the two metals?

Metal 1 _COPPER_

Metal 2 _ZINC_ (2)

ii) Describe what is meant by an alloy.

An alloy is _A mixture of two pure metals. When they are combined they produce a material with different properties to the original._ (4)

iii) The body of the tap is a very complicated shape.

From the list of manufacturing methods given, what process is most suitable for making the tap body?

forging   lost wax casting   extruding   resin casting   vacuum forming

I would make the tap body by _LOST WAX CASTING_ (2)

iv) Brass corrodes in certain circumstances and needs protection.

What process is normally used to protect taps from corrosion? Give the fullest description so that a manufacturer can ask his supplier for the best protection.

1 To protect from corrosion this tap needs to be _____

ELECTRO PLATED

_____ (2)

2 What does corrosion mean?

The way materials are attacked by their environment. Some of the metals will decay — Salts produced. (2)

Examiner comment

This question tests a range of material knowledge by using a familiar object, the taps, as a basis for you to show your understanding.

(ULEAC)

Practice questions

A machine, weighing 20 kN, is to be lifted, and then moved to the upper floor of a factory, using a temporary gantry, as shown in Fig. 4.26.

a) i) Name the force present in the chains when lifting the machine. (1)

ii) Using a labelled diagram, show how the beam will deflect when the machine is lifted, indicating the forces present in it. (3)

iii) Using notes and diagrams, show **one** way in which the deflection of the beam could be accurately measured. (5)

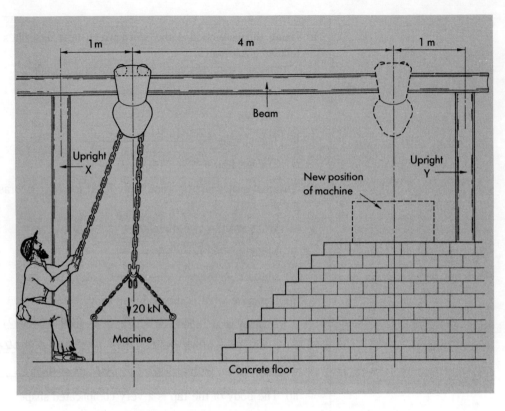

Fig. 4.26

b) Fig. 4.27 shows an enlarged detail of the attachment of the chains to the machine.
   i) Name the force present in the shackle pin.   *(2)*
   ii) Determine the values of the forces in chains A, B and C respectively, when the
       machine is lifted clear of the floor.   *(3)*
   iii) Without using additional chains, describe how the forces in chains B and C could be
        reduced.   *(3)*

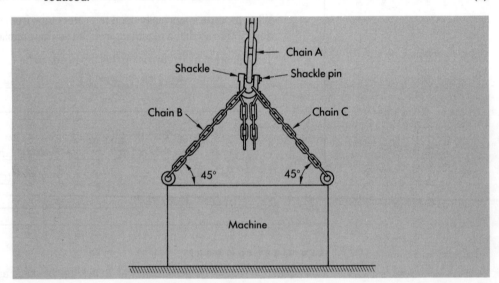

Fig. 4.27

c) The steel used in the gantry is an I section.
   i) Draw and name **three other** suitable steel sections which could be used for the
       beam.   *(6)*
   ii) Show clearly **one** suitable method of joining the beam in Fig. 4.26 to one of the
       uprights.   *(3)*

d) With the pulley block in the position shown in Fig. 4.26 and the machine lifted clear of
   the floor:
   i) Calculate the forces in the uprights **X** and **Y** respectively.   *(4)*
   ii) Draw the shear force diagram, and clearly label the point of maximum shear.   *(4)*
   iii) Draw the bending moment diagram, and determine the value of the maximum
        bending moment.   *(5)*

e) When designing a structure, we usually incorporate a **factor of safety**.
   i) Describe what is meant by the term **factor of safety**. (2)
   ii) Give **three** reasons why a factor of safety is necessary. (3)
   iii) Suggest a suitable factor of safety for the gantry in Fig. 4.26, for the application described. (1)

f) i) Using notes and diagrams, show a suitable construction for the concrete floor in Fig. 4.26. (3)
   ii) Give the names of **two** properties which make concrete a suitable material for the floor. (2)

(Total 50 marks)
(MEG – structures example)

3 a) Give **two** reasons why concrete is so widely used as a structural material.

   i) _____ (1)

   ii) _____ (1)

b) Fig. 4.28 shows a cast concrete beam which is supporting the brickwork above it.

Fig. 4.28

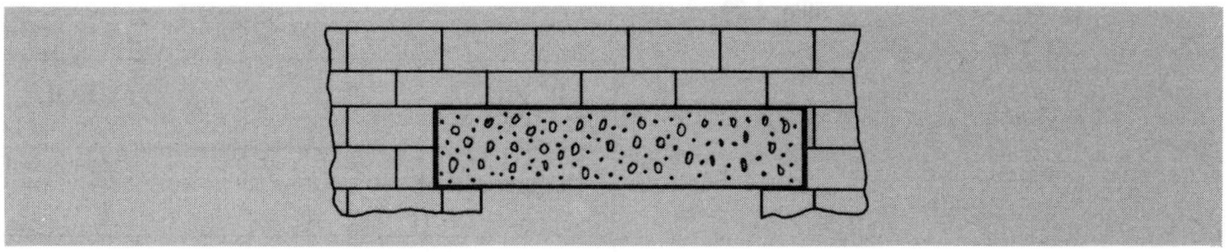

   i) Draw a diagram of the principal loads acting on the beam. (2)

   ii) Mark with a cross the place where the beam is most likely to fail. (1)

   iii) Why does concrete need to be reinforced when it is being made into this type of structure?

   _____

   _____ (1)

   iv) Show on the sketch where steel reinforcing rods should be placed, and explain how this makes the beam stronger.

   Explanation: _____

   _____ (4)
(SEG – structures)

4 a) For each application given in the table state:

   i) a suitable material;
   ii) a property of that material which makes it suitable for that application.

APPLICATION	MATERIAL	PROPERTY
Gears		
Plastic bottles		
Lathe cutting-tools		
Canoe		

(8)

b) i) Explain what is meant by:

Thermoplastic Material:	Thermosetting Material:
_____	_____
_____	_____
_____	_____

ii) State an example of each.

_____   _____

_____   _____

(4)

(SEG – materials)

MECHANISMS

Question 1 and outline answer

Complete the table by using a symbol from the list below (Fig. 4.29) for the motion.

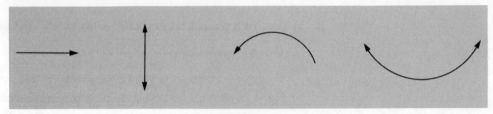

Fig. 4.29

MOTION	SYMBOL
Reciprocating	
Linear	
Oscillating	
Rotary	

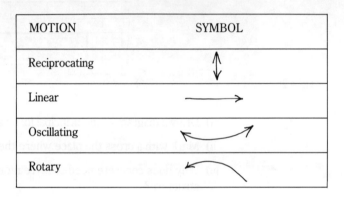

(4)

Examiner comment

A simple question asking you to show an understanding of some basic mechanism notation.

Practice questions

1   Fig. 4.30 shows the plan arrangement of a waterwheel which is to drive a generator for the supply of electricity.

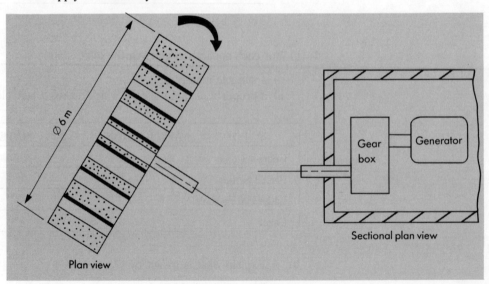

Fig. 4.30

Plan view

Sectional plan view

Gear box

Generator

Ø 6 m

a) The two shafts are not in line. Sketch on Fig. 4.30 a method of solving this problem so that both shafts rotate at the same speed. (3)

b) i) Name and sketch the construction of a suitable type of bearing which could be used to support the waterwheel shaft.

Name of bearing: _____

ii) Give **one** reason why this type of bearing is suitable for this application.

Reason: _____ *(4)*

(SEG)

2 Explain, with the aid of a sketch, how a pawl and ratchet can be used on a wheel and axle to stop a cable from unwinding when it has been wound in a clockwise direction.

(8)

_____

_____

_____

_____

_____

_____

_____

(WJEC)

DIGITAL MICROELECTRONICS

Practice questions

This question is the type often used in the early part of a structured paper.

1 Here you are given the truth table for a logic gate.

A	B	Q
0	0	1
1	0	1
0	1	1
1	1	0

a) i) Complete the diagram (Fig. 4.31) with the symbol of the logic gate described in the truth table.

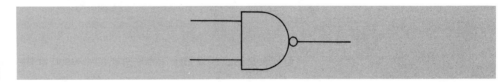

Fig. 4.31

ii) Name the logic gate you have drawn.

_____ *(3)*

b) i) Complete the diagram (Fig. 4.32) showing how the two gates can be connected to form a flip-flop.

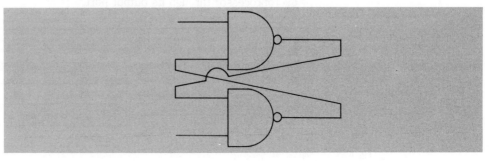

Fig. 4.32

ii) Explain the meaning of the term *flip-flop*.

_____

_____

_____ *(6)*

The following questions show the range of the work in this module from simple logic to computer/microprocessor control.

2   As part of a sales promotion, a manufacturer wishes to give away a battery operated alarm with each freezer sold. The alarm indicates when the freezer door is open. The alarm will fit to the freezer as shown in Fig. 4.33.

Fig. 4.33

a) With notes and sketches show a type of simple sensor which could be fitted to the door to trigger the alarm. *(4)*

b)   i) Complete the circuit diagram in Fig. 4.34 so that the circuit will latch on when the sensor switch is broken.

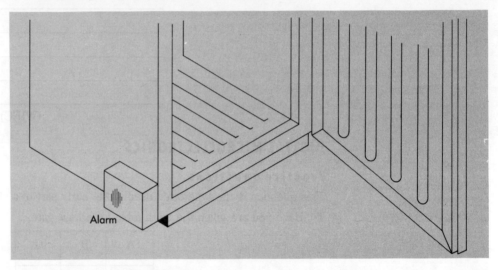

Fig. 4.34

ii) Name the **two** logic gates you have used in the circuit.

_____

_____ *(10)*

(ULEAC)

3   Fig. 4.35 shows how a crane with an electromagnetic pick-up is controlled from a microprocessor through its output port.

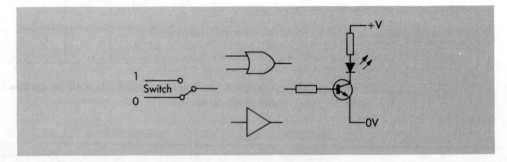

Bit 3	Bit 2	Bit 1	Bit 0	Control of	Logic state 1	Logic state 0
				Motor	On	Off
				Motor	Forward	Reverse
				Electromagnetic	On	Off
				Siren	On	Off

Fig. 4.35

The program to drive the crane requires a number of combinations of signals.
For each of the conditions shown in the table (Fig. 4.36) state the output condition
needed to operate the devices required.   *(8)*
                                                                           (SEG)

	Output Condition	
	(Binary)	
(a) Motor running forward.	□□□□ = decimal	□□□□
(b) Motor running forward, electromagnet on.	□□□□ = decimal	□□□□
(c) Motor running reverse, siren on	□□□□ = decimal	□□□□
(d) Motor running forward, siren on	□□□□ = hexadecimal	□□□□

Fig. 4.36

PNEUMATICS

Practice questions

1 A block diagram pneumatic time delay circuit for the opening and closing of a car park
barrier is shown in Fig. 4.37.

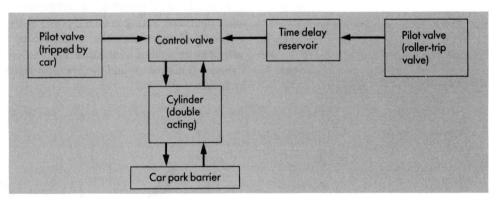

Fig. 4.37

Using British Standard graphical symbols, draw a pneumatic circuit diagram for the car
park barrier.   *(8)*
                                                                          (WJEC)

2 In this question you are being asked to show a working knowledge of a simple
pneumatic circuit. The question also tests your ability to draw appropriate circuit
symbols. Again it helps if you draw your circuit clearly.

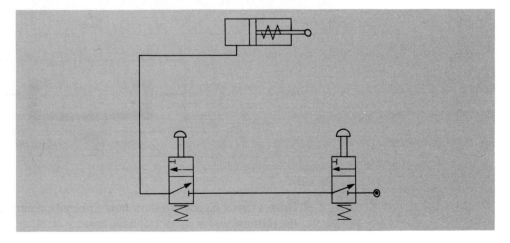

Fig. 4.38

In Fig. 4.38 you are shown the partly completed circuit diagram for a trimming guillotine used at one point in the food processing plant. The blade of the guillotine is operated when the cylinder goes positive. For safety reasons the cylinder must only go positive if both the push-button-operated three port valves are operated.

a) Complete the circuit diagram.   (6)

b) Explain what is meant by the cylinder going positive.

_____

_____ (1)

c) Name the logic circuit formed by this arrangement of three port valves.

_____ (1)

(ULEAC)

3 a) Give **two** uses of compressed air in a garage workshop.   (2)

b) Using clear diagrams and brief notes, explain the difference between the construction and operation of SINGLE ACTING and DOUBLE ACTING cylinders.   (6)

Fig. 4.39 illustrates a pressing machine which folds thin sheet steel in two stages, using double acting cylinders.

Stage 1 – Cylinder **A** outstrokes to press the sheet into a U shape by pushing the material between the jaws which are fitted to cylinders **B** and **C**. When cylinder **A** has completed its outstroke, the support platform is then touching the machine base, and the spring is fully compressed.

Stage 2 – Cylinders **B** and **C** outstroke simultaneously to form the folded ends, hitting roller operated, spring return 3-port valves at the end of their strokes.

Stage 3 – Cylinders **B** and **C** instroke, hitting roller operated, spring return 3-port valves at the end of their strokes.

Stage 4 – Cylinder **A** instrokes, and the operator removes the formed piece of metal by hand.

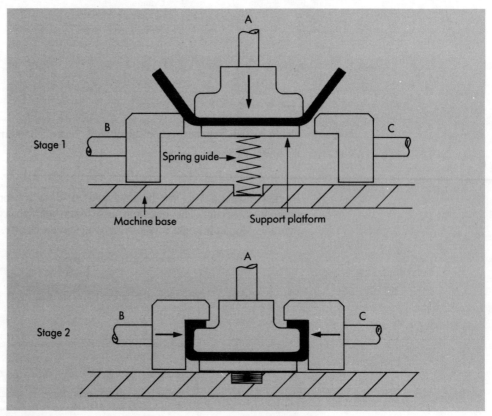

Fig. 4.39

c) Draw a circuit diagram to show how air bleed circuitry could be used to sense when the platform was in contact with the base.   (6)

d) The folding sequence previously described is achieved in the following way:
   - sheet metal placed in the machine by the operator;
   - safety guard closed by the operator, the guard activates a plunger operated, spring return 3-port valve. The machine will not operate unless this guard is closed;
   - operator presses a button operated, spring return 3-port valve to start the folding sequence described.

Draw a flow chart to show the complete sequence.   (8)
                                                                                (MEG)

A FINAL STATEMENT

- Remember the optional modules are a small element of your course.
- Much of what you need to know you will have practised through your design and practical work.
- The questions will ask you to show understanding and application of your knowledge to problems.

CHAPTER 5

COURSEWORK

HOW ASSESSMENT WORKS

FINDING A PROJECT

HOW THE PROJECT IS ASSESSED

MANAGING A PROJECT

GETTING STARTED

Your coursework is the most important part of your GCSE CDT: Technology course. No matter which syllabus you are taking your coursework will form at least 45% of your final mark.

CENTRE ASSESSED PROJECT(S)

50% of the total marks have been allocated to this component on the Examination: the actual marks given to candidates will be scaled to this allocation.

The Coursework component of the Examination provides the major opportunity for candidates to show their abilities in a linked sequence of designing, making, and evaluating, that integrates the learning, of both skills and knowledge, acquired during the course. Each candidate will be expected to submit a project or projects for assessment that have been carried out in the last two full terms of the year of the Examination. It is anticipated that a candidate's project will occupy up to a total of 45 hours of class time. The teacher should encourage all candidates to base this work on any relevant personal interest or area of experience, and candidates should be encouraged to seek information from any appropriate source. A choice of project(s) should be made which will enable candidates to show evidence of positive achievement even if they attain only the earlier levels of the assessment criteria.

(SEG)

You should, therefore, spend the largest part of your time on this aspect of the course. In CDT: Technology examinations coursework usually takes the form of a terminal project or projects. This means that *you* undertake the designing, making, testing and evaluating of a major project during the last three terms of your course.

Some examination groups allow you to submit two smaller projects instead of one major project. WJEC requires you to do two mini projects as part of your work in the optional modules (10% of coursework marks for each project) and one major project (30% of coursework marks).

ESSENTIAL PRINCIPLES

Exactly what you do must be negotiated with your teacher and must meet the requirements of your examination. If you wish you can work in groups but it is important that each member of the group meets the assessment requirements of the examination.

1 > HOW ASSESSMENT WORKS

For assessment your work is marked by your teacher, during and at the end of the course. During the course your teacher will talk to you about how you are doing. This gives you the opportunity to improve your work and your final assessment. Your teacher's assessment is finally moderated by the Examining Group. Sometimes this means that someone will visit your school and look at some or all of the pupils' coursework. Your coursework will be assessed by your teacher and then moderated by an external examiner.

While you can research your project and seek help from a variety of sources, it is important that the work is your own.

To do well you must thoroughly **plan** and **organise** your work over a long period. Usually the final project occupies most of your time during the last three terms of the course.

In your final coursework project and in any mini projects which form part of your coursework, you will have to show the use of the full design process. Your design work will be presented in a folio or design folder, which must show:

- How you identified the need from a situation or context.
- The design brief to which you worked.
- How you analysed the problems.
- The alternative ideas you began to develop.
- Models of some of your ideas.
- Why you decided upon the final ideas you were going to develop.
- A series of working drawings and material specifications for your final idea.
- Details of manufacture and any modifications you made.
- How you tested the finished product.
- The evaluation of the finished product against your original design criteria.

66 Elements in your design folder. 99

Remember. In your coursework you have both the time and freedom to use whatever means of communication is most suitable to the problem you are solving. Fig. 5.1 shows two completely contrasting methods of presentation.

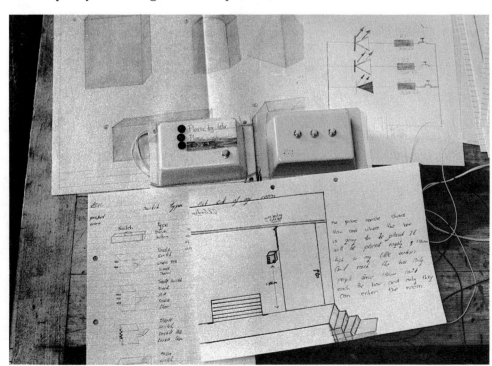

Fig. 5.1 You can choose the means of communicating your ideas and work

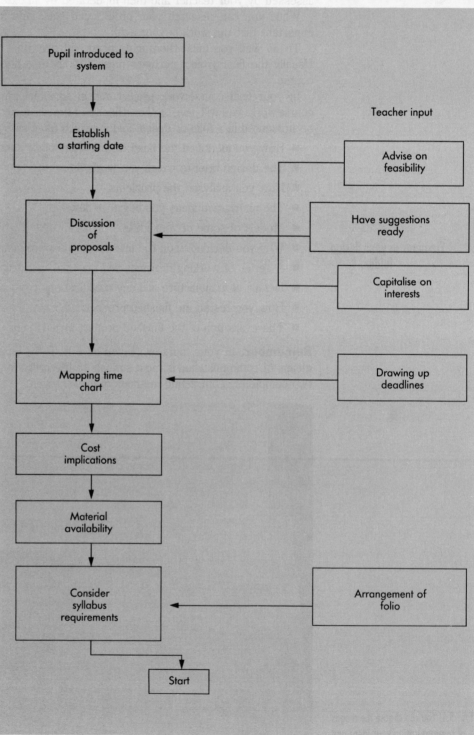

Fig. 5.2 Guidance for the planning of projects

You will do well with your coursework if you:

- Start to think about a project well before you have to start work upon it.
- Talk to your teacher about your ideas. Try to decide upon a project in which you are interested and which is within your capabilities.
- Make sure your project covers all the assessment objectives in the coursework part of the syllabus.

Hints for doing well in coursework

- Make sure the amount of work in your project is realistic for the time you have. Remember the other GCSE subjects you are doing will also have a coursework element.
- Keep a project log to show whether you are keeping up to date with your work.
- Make sure you know the date when you must finish by. Use your project log to set yourself targets.
- See your project as a partnership between you and your teacher.

The chart (Fig. 5.2) outlines some of these points.

It is important to use this chapter together with chapter 3 – Design. In this chapter we will look at:

- Finding a project.
- How the project is assessed.
- Managing a project.

2 > FINDING A PROJECT

Often before you start to think of a project for GCSE you will ask the question:

'What is a suitable project for the examination?'

This is very difficult to answer and will depend upon a range of factors:

- Your ability and experience – how well are you doing on the course?
  - did you do a CDT Foundation course?
  - are you taking other GCSE subjects which help your CDT: Technology?
- Do you have to work with one teacher only?
- Which optional modules have you studied?

Points to bear in mind when finding a project.

- Will you be able to have any outside (e.g. industrial) assistance/advice with your project?
- What facilities and materials do you have available?
- How much time can you give?
- Will there be a cost limit on your project?
- Does your idea meet the aims and assessment objectives of the syllabus you are taking?
- Do you feel you are able to do the project you have chosen?

All of these factors must be considered **before** you start any project. The answers will obviously be dependent upon your own ideas and interests, what your school offers and the choices your teachers make. So it is almost impossible to give suggestions of suitable projects. Of course, providing your project meets the aims and assessment objectives of the syllabus you are taking, then it **is** suitable. If you have any doubts, your teacher will advise you. Some examining groups produce a sample project list to give you some ideas, though these lists are not seen as exclusive. Have a look through the list below.

LIST OF SELECTED MAJOR PRACTICAL PROJECTS

This list is not intended to be prescriptive or exhaustive; it is offered simply as an indication of the wide range of possibilities for practical projects.

PNEUMATIC

1	**Metalwork or jewellery vice**	pneumatically operated by one or two double acting cylinders.
2	**Car park barrier**	pneumatic operation – coin operating mechanism – automatically closing after car has passed.
3	**Plastic forming press**	pneumatic press to form plastic trays, dishes or containers.
4	**Food slicer**	pneumatically controlled machine to slice food – cheese, fruit, bread.
5	**Hackshaw**	pneumatic hacksaw machine – possible pneumatic vice.
6	**Drinks dispenser**	machine to dispense fruit drinks automatically.
7	**Combination door lock**	a number of air bleeds which, when covered in the correct combination, open a door.
8	**Automatic door opener**	door mat triggers pressure sensitive valve.
9	**Automatic can opener**	machine to open beer or soft drink cans automatically.
10	**Automatic control of lathe**	cross slide feed – power from pneumatic cylinders – detection circuits.
11	**Lathe turret control**	pneumatic control of a lathe turret head to rotate lathe tools.
12	**Fabric tester**	fatigue test for fabrics – wire brush on pneumatic cylinder.
13	**Automatic control of drill press**	power tool drill with sequential controlled feed and vice.
14	**Pneumatic shaper**	shaping machine operated by pneumatic cylinder.
15	**Rocking horse**	GRP body of horse with pneumatic driven mechanism – suitable for children's playground.
16	**Printing press**	pneumatic printing press – sequential control to feed paper and operate press.
17	**Joint testing machine**	pneumatic machine for testing woodwork joints.
18	**Fluidic control**	fluidic control of any device such as a coin-in-the-slot dispenser of drinks or sweets.
19	**Flower watering device**	pneumatic device to water pot plants automatically.
20	**Guinness pouring machine**	pneumatic machine to take cap off bottle and pour from bottle.

ELECTRONIC

1	**Automatic counting device**	device to count people entering a room – possible use of photocells or photo transistors.
2	**Burglar alarm**	could be photocell device, or infra-red detector, micro switches, multivibrator alarm.
3	**Garage door opener**	automatically opens garage doors when motor car approaches.
4	**Smoke detector**	fire alarm to detect smoke.
5	**Rain alarm**	to detect when it is raining and wind in washing line.
6	**Amplifier**	for record player or cassette player or guitar – or as an intercom.
7	**Binary counter**	electronic machine to count in binary, with possible denary decoding.
8	**Electronic organ**	investigation of wave shapes and frequency from electronic organ using discrete components or integrated circuits.
9	**Frequency selective amplifier**	amplifier to control fluctuations of light in time with the frequency of musical input.

ELECTRICAL

1	**Bicycle ergonometer**	to determine power and efficiency of human body, using a bicycle.
2	**Plant propagator**	control of soil heating unit in greenhouse.

| 3 **Model railway controller** | transformer, rectifier, speed control. |
| 4 **Battery charger** | power supply to charge car batteries with thermal overload facility. |

INSTRUMENTATION

1 **Automatic weather station**	a) anemometer to measure wind speed – possible analogue or digital display.
	b) wind direction indicator, possibly using LED's for display.
	c) measuring rainfall – possible use of strain gauges.
	d) measuring temperature – electronic thermometer using thermistor or diode or transistor to sense temperature.
2 **Solar heater**	instrumentation of temperature fluctuation and recording.
3 **Tachometer**	to measure speed of rotation of lathe, or electric motor of kart engine – possible analogue or digital display.
4 **Measuring liquid level**	measuring to level of liquid in a tank – inflammable liquids, possible analogue or digital display.
5 **Seismograph**	device to record earthquakes or vibrations of traffic near motorway.
6 **Temperature measurement of casting metal**	to measure the temperature of molten metal used for casting in a school foundry.

MECHANICAL

1 **Coil winding machine**	a mechanical device to wind solenoid coils – possibly count number of turns and lay the wire evenly on the coil.
2 **Self steering device**	programmed mechanical vehicle that steers a predetermined course.
3 **Brake design for a kart**	design for a mechanical braking system on a kart.
4 **Toggle or cam press**	press to operate punch tools with toggle or cam or linkage action.
5 **Index machine**	device to index Hybridex strip through the drilling machine with ½″ indexing between holes.
6 **Weighing machine**	use of linkages to provide weighing machine mechanism – calibration.
7 **Vehicle**	model of vehicle steering suspension.
8 **Mechanical counting machine**	device to count tablets mechanically.

(NEAB)

Further examples of suitable problems

1 A manufacturer needs to check if certain components on a production line are overweight. He wants to eject components that are too heavy but allow correct or underweight components to continue.

2 A roll of cartridge paper requires cutting accurately into equal lengths. The system can be started manually for each length of paper. The operator's safety is important.

3 A marksman shoots at a rifle target that is 25 metres away. He gets tired of walking up to the target to see if he has hit the bullseye. He is looking for a system that will indicate when he has scored on the bullseye only.

4 DIY enthusiasts often use electric drills on the floors or walls of their homes and are quite likely to puncture electric cables or cental heating pipes. A system is needed to avoid this.

5 A disabled person, paralysed from the waist down, is often extremely strong in the arms. Canoeing would be a very popular sport for such a person if he could eject safely from the canoe cockpit.

6 Rockclimbers often spend their holidays on big mountains. Very seldom do they have the access to accurate localised weather forecasting that is necessary for safety.

7   School office staff are forever duplicating paper and counting it into batches for distribution to class groups. A lot of time and tedium would be saved if this process could be speeded up.

8   A manufacturer needs to automate a steam bending process with timber. He needs an "S" shaped length but finds that if he uses a simple clamping system it is difficult to prevent the timber moving lengthwise in the mould. He has to allow for this movement by using longer lengths than necessary and trim them up later. He would like to avoid this wastage each time.

9   A BMX racing enthusiast has to transport his bike to race meetings by car. He is looking for a reliable lightweight structure that could be clamped to an ordinary commercial roofrack.

10 A pupil who is keen on graphics wants a cheap airbrush system into which he can locate ordinary jumbo felt tip pens rather than the highly priced commercial alternatives.

11 People not long out of hospital, or the elderly, often have to take regular medication in the form of tablets. Being ill, they can easily forget what they have done and take an overdose. They need a dispenser that "remembers" when they took a tablet last.

Questions for consideration by candidates

These questions have been devised to assist candidates in preparing their project reports.

1   What is the title of your project?

2   What is your project brief?

3   Why did you choose this particular project?

4   Where did the idea for your project come from? (Teacher's suggestion; magazine search; something that you had read; TV; or something original.)

5   Have you considered other ways of solving your problem?

6   Have you considered the cost, in terms of time, equipment availability, of your project? How has this affected your final solution?

7   Have you set down a detailed specification for your project saying what it will do (and possibly what it will not do), over what range and what its requirements are?

8   Have you considered how you are going to test your project?

9   Have you the equipment to do this testing?

10 Will your project be safe for someone else to use? **Note: No accessible part of your project may be at mains voltage.**

11 How have you ensured your project is safe?

12 Have you made a timetable for the completion of your project?

13 Are there any special properties of the materials you have chosen which make them particularly suitable for your project?

14 How do you intend to present your final project? Will labelling/instructions be needed so that others can operate your project as you intend?

15 Is it going to be necessary for you to build prototypes?

16 Are you going to need to use any facilities from another department (e.g. a lathe if you work mainly in a science laboratory, or electrical meters etc. if you work mainly in a craft department)? Can this be arranged?

17 Will all parts of your project be readily accessible for testing and modification should it be necessary?

18 Have you considered how colour coding may help explain what you are doing?

19 Have you made sketches of parts of your construction to explain particularly important features?

20 Have you illustrated the tests you have carried out to check whether your project met its specification?

21 Have you made lists or tables of readings from the tests? Were they what you expected?

22 In the event of a problem, have you written details of checks on individual sections?

23 If you wish to make modifications to your project at this stage, what evidence can you provide of what you have achieved so far? Photographs, Sketches?

24 Have you listed the sources of ideas and information you have used such as magazines, books, teacher, etc? (Include name, author, publisher and page number.) **This is essential**.

25 Would it be clear from your project record that you have written the report in stages, as you have gone along, rather than after completion and evaluation of the project?

26 Have you tested the reliability of your project?

27 With hindsight, what aspects, if any, would you undertake differently if you were tackling the same project again?

(NEAB)

Perhaps the most important factor you must consider is **time**. Remember this is not the only GCSE subject in which you have to complete coursework.

LEAG have given the following guideline:

'However, the major limitation is time and it is important that pupils spend about 45 hours of classwork time on the major project. This equates to a four-period-per-week block, each period of around half an hour's duration, for twenty-two and a half weeks of term time.'

This is seen as a **minimum** requirement for a successful project; you may well spend a lot more time working on your coursework.

Once you have considered this range of factors, then you need to carefully **identify** the project or projects you will attempt. In chapter 3 on Design (pages 22–3) we looked at how you could identify a *need* from a *context* and then begin to design a solution.

To identify a project you need a context or situation. This may be provided by the teacher or by use of visits, video or by direct inputs to the students from outside agencies. From this context individual or group problems can be identified by the students. This process must be seen as a joint exercise with the teacher guiding but the decisions remaining with the pupils. At this stage pupils can identify the specific need and design brief to which they will work. The process is shown in diagram form in Fig. 5.3.

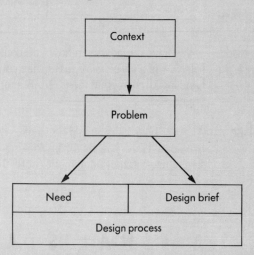

Fig. 5.3

Whilst some students will reach a point where they will be able to use this process with little or no teacher guidance, others will require assistance at various stages. Throughout the process, it is important to ensure that pupils are presented with tasks appropriate to their individual levels of ability. This, again, is emphasised in the syllabus.

(ULEAC)

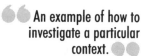 **It is worth spending time at the very beginning.**

As you can see from the LEAG statement, the *process* of identifying a project involves a lot of work before you even begin to start solving the need. Throughout this process it is important that what you are doing is suitable for your experience and ability. Do not try to do something which is far too difficult for you. Again, your teacher will advise you.

The following is an example of how you could begin to investigate a *context* to identify a need, which could become your project.

An example of how to investigate a particular context.

If we look at the **family** as the context, you have several ways to start investigating:

■ Choose a **part of your home** – see how everyone uses it – kitchen, garage, greenhouse, bedroom, etc.

■ identify any problems which each user has:
– Mum wants to know if the freezer door has been left open.
– Granny has a problem with holding knives and other kitchen utensils.

■ Do these provide any suitable starting points for a project?

OR

- Choose a **member of the family** – sister/brother – younger/older – mother/father/grandparents.
- identify a need they have – could this provide a suitable project?

If you use this approach it may help to prepare some simple checklists, like the ones shown below in Figs 5.4 and 5.5.

TASK	EASY			DIFFICULT		PERSON GRANNY
Cutting vegetables	1	2	3	④	5	
Opening Tins	1	2	3	④	5	
Opening Bottles	1	2	3	④	5	
Holding Saucepans	1	2	③	4	5	

Fig. 5.4 Scoring tasks in terms of difficulty

TASK	OPENING FREEZER	TOTAL
Mum	╫╫ I	6
Dad	II	2
Brother	IIII	4
Sister	╫╫ II	7
Granny	IIII	4

Fig. 5.5 Frequency chart of tasks

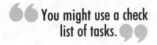 **You might use a check list of tasks.**

We have already seen how you could use a simple *questionnaire* to help identify a need. Fig. 5.4 is a *checklist of tasks* that you might use in questions to a person (here 'granny') handling kitchen equipment etc. A simple means of 'scoring' the replies to your questions is suggested.

You could use a frequency chart.

Another possibility would be to use a *frequency chart*, shown in Fig. 5.5, to help identify a problem. Here you might be looking at the number of times different members of your family use kitchen equipment (here the freezer) in a given period of time.

A FINAL STATEMENT

- Finding a project is very important.
- It has to be started well before the final year of your course.
- It will take longer than you think.
- The project you choose must be within your capabilities and meet the aims and assessment objectives of the syllabus you are taking.
- Talk to your teacher about your project ideas.

3 ▷ HOW THE PROJECT IS ASSESSED

Your coursework is worth up to 50% of your final mark. It is the one point in your course when you can improve your assessment over a period of time by improving or adding to your work. It is therefore important to know exactly how, and on what, you will be assessed.

The mark-scheme is an important guide to your work.

Again if you look at the syllabus you are taking, you will find an assessment scheme for the final project. This is what your teacher will use to mark your project.

The mark scheme will usually be broken down into *specific skills* – here we look at the MEG mark scheme for 'Investigation and Research'.

Investigation and research

a) **Low Achievement (0–15)**
   i) Little or no evidence of investigation or research submitted. When a selection is made, only one solution considered or attempted.   0–7
   ii) Some evidence of research, with superficial evidence of investigation or reading about the problem.
   An attempt to consider two solutions but one rejected for flimsy or unstated reasons.   8–15

b) **Medium Achievement (16–30)**
   i) Bottom of this range, some real research and investigation with poor presentation of results.   16–22
   ii) Some good research and investigation into the problem.
   Results presented with some use of supporting illustrative material.
   Some consideration of three solutions with weak evidence for the rejection of two of them.   23–30

c) **High Achievement (31–45)**
   i) Some good research and investigation into the problem. Results well presented with good use of supporting illustrative material. In depth consideration of three or more solutions – two rejected for good stated reasons.   31–37
   ii) Full evidence of good sound research and investigation into the problem. Good selection, presentation of data and/or organisation of experiments with very full well written up and presented supporting work and conclusions. Three or more solutions considered in great depth with good reasons for rejecting alternatives clearly and concisely stated.   38–45

(MEG Mark Scheme – Investigation and Research)

Some of the assessment schemes, like the one above, use a *range of marks* for each statement – i.e. specific aspects of a skill. Others, like the one below for LEAG, use a *specific mark* for each statement – here the skill is 'Realisation', broken down into a variety of specific aspects or statements. These statements are called *criteria* and are what your project will be judged against.

Realisation

i) Selection of Resources
The candidate has demonstrated an ability to:
a) select resources from a wider range, which is familiar to her or him: 1
b) select resources from a wider range, making reference to suitability: 2
c) select resources from a wider range, making reference to suitability in terms of cost and availability: 3
d) select resources from a wider range, after considering suitability in terms of cost and availability: 4
e) select resources from a range, which is both familiar and unfamiliar; make judgements about suitability in terms of cost and availability: 5
f) select resources from a range, which is both familiar and unfamiliar; make judgements about suitability after examining cost and availability: 6
g) select resources from a range, which is both familiar and unfamiliar; make judgements about suitability after investigating properties and examining cost and availability.   7

ii) Plan for Production
The candidate has:
a) produced no plans for the production of the final design and has used simple processes in an unrelated order to partly complete the solution.   1
b) produced simple plans for the production of the final design and has used different but unrelated stages to nearly complete the solution: 2
c) produced simple plans for the production of the final design and has used different stages in a related order to plan the complete solution: 3
d) produced outline plans for the production of the final design in related stages, in an order that would lead to a partly completed solution: 4
e) produced outline plans including the plans for the production of the final design in related stages, which would lead to a nearly completed solution.   5

f) produced plans, which show some detail, both of process and time, for the production of the final design in related stages, which provide an ordered progression and would enable a solution to be produced: 6

g) produced detailed plans for the production of the final design in related stages, which provide a logical progression and would enable a completed solution to be produced in a time scale. 7

iii) Manipulative Skills

The candidate has demonstrated the ability to:

a) use simple manipulative skills to produce a limited realisation: 3

b) use simple manipulative skills to produce an artefact or system which simply relates to the proposed solution: 6

c) use simple manipulative skills to produce an artefact or system which relates to the proposed solution: 9

d) use particular manipulative skills in a competent manner to produce an artefact or system which is close to the basic aspects of the proposed solution: 12

e) use manipulative skills in a competent manner to produce an artefact or system which is close to main aspects of the proposed solution: 15

f) use accurate manipulative skills to produce an artefact or system, in which the details shown in the proposed solution can be clearly identified. 18

(ULEAC mark scheme – Realisation)

Whichever of the examining group's syllabuses you are taking the assessment scheme is broadly the same. Fig. 5.6 below shows a comparison of the assessment areas used by each exam group.

GROUP				
ULEAC	**MEG**	**NEAB**	**SEG**	**WJEC**
Project brief	Title, Introduction, Description, Specification, Analysis, Planning of the problem	Recognition of problem	Identification and analysis of the problem	Brief
Analysis of problem		Analysis of problem		Investigations
Proposed solutions		Research/testing	Specification of performance	Development of solutions
Selection of proposed solution	Investigation and research	Specification	Investigation, research and experimentation	Final solution
		Generation of ideas		Evaluation
Development of final design	Technical quality of finished work		Generation of possible solutions and ideas for development	
	Fitness for purpose	Solution		
Realisation ↓		Presentation of report		
Selection of resources	Testing and evaluation	Evaluations	Selection of an appropriate solution	
Plan for production			Technical design	
Manipulative skills			Design and planning of practical realisation	
Evaluation			Quality of manufacture construction and assembly	
			Performance	

| GROUP | | | | |
ULEAC	MEG	NEAB	SEG	WJEC
A R E A S O F A S S E S S M E N T			Testing of performance and modifications	
			Evaluation	
			Organisation and presentation of the report	

Fig. 5.6 Project assessment table

As you can see your assessment will be based on five main areas.

- Identifying a need.
- Designing a solution.
- Planning.
- Making.
- Evaluating.

This is very important and means that your work must be a combination of making your project, and recording how you:

- identified it,
- designed it,
- modified it, and
- evaluated it.

Your project report or folio is as important as what you make. You need both if you are to do well on your final project. Use the information in Chapter 3 – Design, to help you with presenting your project report or folio.

Ask your teacher for a copy of the *assessment scheme*. Again, as with the subject content of the course, use it as a check list to see when you have achieved the particular assessment criteria. Use it initially to make sure that your project will cover **all** of the assessment areas.

From time to time, ask your teacher to give you an assessment on what you have done. Ask how you could improve your assessment. Remember, few people will do well at every point in the assessment scheme. Try to ensure that you do as well as you can, especially in areas where you know your strengths are. For example, if you are very good at making things, then you should get a good assessment on the making aspects of the assessment scheme.

A FINAL STATEMENT

■ The coursework assessment is one of the most important parts of your CDT: Technology course.

■ To do well you need to know how and on what you will be assessed. Ask your teacher for advice.

■ Remember the assessment will include your project report or folio and what you make.

■ Few people are able to do well in every single aspect of the project assessment scheme.

4 ＞ MANAGING A PROJECT

It is vital that you keep control of your project.

Your final project will occupy a major part of the final three school terms of your CDT: Technology course. When you first consider your project there always seems to be a long time from when you start to when you have to finish. Your teacher may well start talking to you about the final project well over a year before you take the formal examination parts of your course. In fact the time goes very quickly and most candidates have to work hard to finish in the time available.

Also, you have to ensure that your project and its report covers all of the aspects required in the scheme of assessment.

If you are going to achieve this and keep to the time limits of your course, it helps to have some simple system to **manage** your project. The following suggestions are some simple ways in which you can keep control of your project and know what you are doing. They will also help your teacher to see where you are with your project, and can even count towards your assessment.

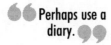

Perhaps use a diary.

■ Keep and use a simple project *diary*, like the one shown below in Fig. 5.7.

Target	Work done
Week End October 12th Complete the P.C.B. transfer and prepare the board for etching.	Completed all of the P.C.B. work. Checked with my teacher about ordering components.
Week End October 19th Complete the P.C.B board begin drilling.	Completed the board. Didn't start drilling. Components have arrived.

Fig. 5.7 Simple project diary

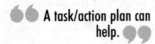

A task/action plan can help.

■ If you work in a group, or as an individual, try using a *task/action plan* to help plan your work. (Fig. 5.8)

■ Another way to control and manage your project is to use a *flowchart*. The example in Fig. 5.9 is just one way of looking at the problem as a whole.

Fig. 5.8 Task/action plan

PROJECT:								
TASK	ACTION							
	TEAM MEMBER							
	David	Jane	Michael	Susan				
Design Process	✓	✓	✓	✓				
Plan for manufacture	✓		✓					
Making Stage 1	✓			✓				
Stage 2		✓	✓					
Testing								

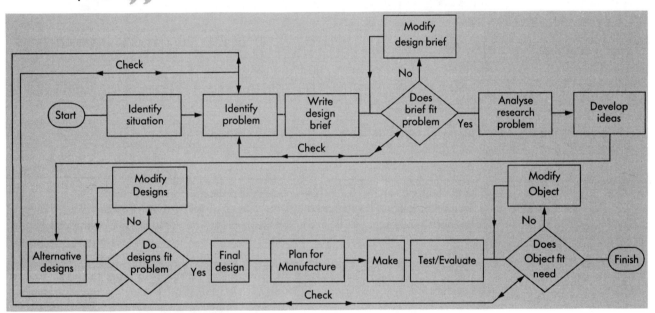

66 **Flowcharts help you look at the whole problem.** 99

Fig. 5.9 Flowchart for planning your project work

■ Fig. 5.10 presents a *time plan*. Such a plan can be a vital part of project planning. You can fill this one in to help with your current project, if you wish.

TIME PLAN				
STAGES	ESTIMATE		ACTUAL	
	START	FINISH	START	FINISH
Survey situation				
Write & agree brief				
Analyse the problem				
Seek additional informations				
Books/Catalogues				
Library				
Letter				
Ask people				
Experiment				
Other				
Design 1				
2				
3				

66 **A time-plan is vital.** 99

Fig. 5.10 Time plan

TIME PLAN

STAGES	ESTIMATE		ACTUAL	
	START	FINISH	START	FINISH
Criticism				
Final design				
Cost				
Plan for manufacture				
Manufacture part 1				
2				
3				
4				
5				
Assemble				
Test				
Evaluate				
Modify				
Re-test				
Final evaluation				

Project: ———————————————— Name: ——————————

The photographs in Fig. 5.11 show a variety of projects. You must ensure that your project is well recorded and documented in your folio or project report. You can use a variety of techniques (see pages 34–9) but it is essential that you communicate your ideas clearly.

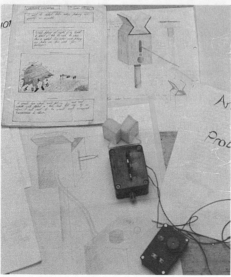

Fig. 5.11 Project work

A   F I N A L   S T A T E M E N T

A final project is spread over a long period of time and involves many activities.
If these are to be successful you need some way of checking:

- what you have done,
- where you are,
- what is still to be done.

Remember. Managing your project is part of planning and is part of your assessment.

SUBJECT CONTENT

MATERIAL RESOURCES AND STRUCTURES

WORKING PROPERTIES OF MATERIALS

FORCES

ENERGY

CONTROL SYSTEMS – MECHANICAL AND ELECTRICAL

TECHNOLOGY IN SOCIETY

GETTING STARTED

Throughout all aspects of your course you will need to know and understand a basic *subject content*. This will form the basis of your CDT: Technology *knowledge*, which will be enhanced by the knowledge you gain in your specialist modules. You will use this, together with your design and making skills, in your Coursework, your written examination (particularly the Common Core) and in your Design examination, if your syllabus has one.

The general areas of knowledge which you need to be familiar with are:

- Material Resources and Structures.
- Energy.
- Control systems – mechanical and electrical.
- Technology in society.

Whilst the **titles** of the areas of knowledge are not necessarily the same in the various exam boards, the broad range of knowledge has much in common.

ESSENTIAL PRINCIPLES

This knowledge will be acquired throughout your course and you should be able to become very familiar with it, especially as you will **use** it in the various aspects of your course.

Fig. 6.1 gives an example of the use of basic *material knowledge* in a design solution.

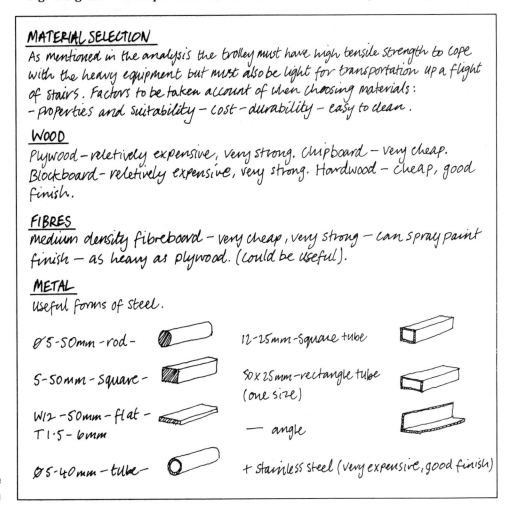

Fig. 6.1 Use of material knowledge in a design solution

Fig. 6.2 illustrates the use of *mechanical knowledge* within a design solution, and Fig. 6.3 the use of *electrical and mechanical* knowledge.

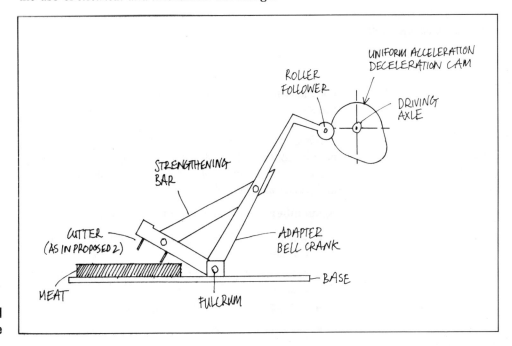

Fig. 6.2 Use of mechanical knowledge

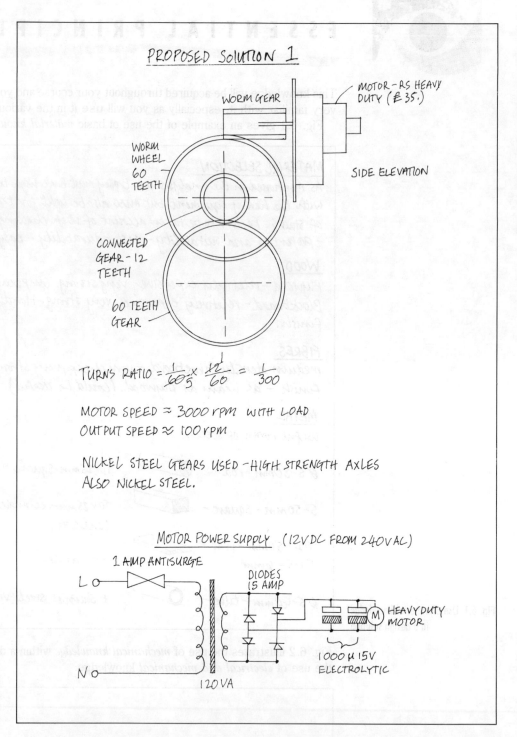

PROPOSED SOLUTION 1

WORM GEAR

MOTOR – RS HEAVY DUTY (£35.)

SIDE ELEVATION

WORM WHEEL 60 TEETH

CONNECTED GEAR – 12 TEETH

60 TEETH GEAR

TURNS RATIO $= \dfrac{1}{60_5} \times \dfrac{12}{60} = \dfrac{1}{300}$

MOTOR SPEED $\approx$ 3000 rPM WITH LOAD
OUTPUT SPEED $\approx$ 100 rPM

NICKEL STEEL GEARS USED – HIGH STRENGTH AXLES
ALSO NICKEL STEEL.

MOTOR POWER SUPPLY (12VDC FROM 240VAC)

1 AMP ANTISURGE

L

DIODES
(5 AMP

HEAVY DUTY
MOTOR

N

120 VA

1000 μ 15V
ELECTROLYTIC

Fig. 6.3 Use of electrical and mechanical knowledge in a design solution

These areas of knowledge are very important and together with your design and communication skills and your making skills can help you gain a high proportion of your marks. Remember, such 'general' areas of knowledge are at least as important as specialist knowledge modules, which only contribute some 20%–30% of your final mark.

Some of the subject content in this chapter will also help your specialist modules. You need to consider the material in this chapter along with that in Chapters 3, 4 and 5. In this chapter we will look at Material Resources and Structures; Energy; Control – mechanical and electrical; Technology in Society.

Remember. To do well in your course you:

■ will need to have a good understanding of the basic CDT: Technology subject content;

■ must be able to use and apply this knowledge in your coursework, written papers and design work;

■ will need to have a set of working notes for this knowledge;

■ will need to become very familiar with this knowledge.

MATERIAL RESOURCES AND STRUCTURES

> **Useful types of material knowledge.**

Throughout the whole of your course you will be providing solutions to problems. All of these solutions will require you to show a range of knowledge about the *materials* you use:

- the way they are formed;
- their working properties;
- the forces which act upon them;
- the forms in which you can obtain them.

In addition, you will need to know **how to use** these materials in any structure which you make. You must be able to make the structure so that the materials can withstand the forces acting upon them.

All of the objects we use, and those that you design and make, are made from a *combination* of materials. Fig. 6.4 shows examples of different projects using a range of different materials.

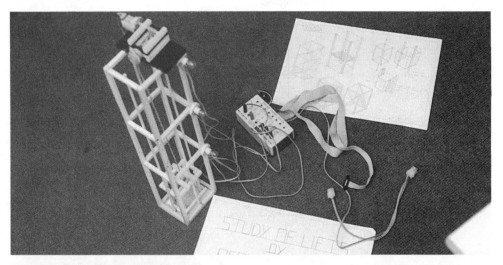

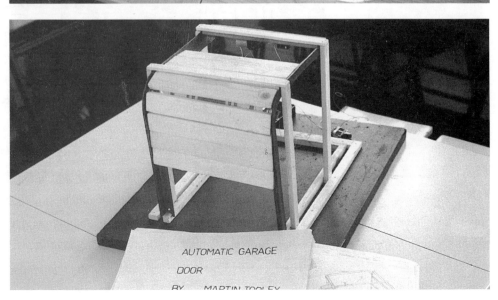

Fig. 6.4 Projects using a range of materials

The materials in these objects are formed by three methods:

- Rearranging.
- Addition.
- Subtraction.

REARRANGING

Here the material is formed into the shape we want. It is rearranged into its shape by pouring, pressing or squeezing into, or against, a mould. No new material is added. Often, particularly with plastics, heat is used to soften the material before moulding. In some situations, such as casting metal, the material is made into a liquid and poured into the mould to form its new shape.

Fig. 6.5 shows a variety of techniques which you can use to shape different materials by rearranging.

> 66 Rearranging is an important method for forming material. 99

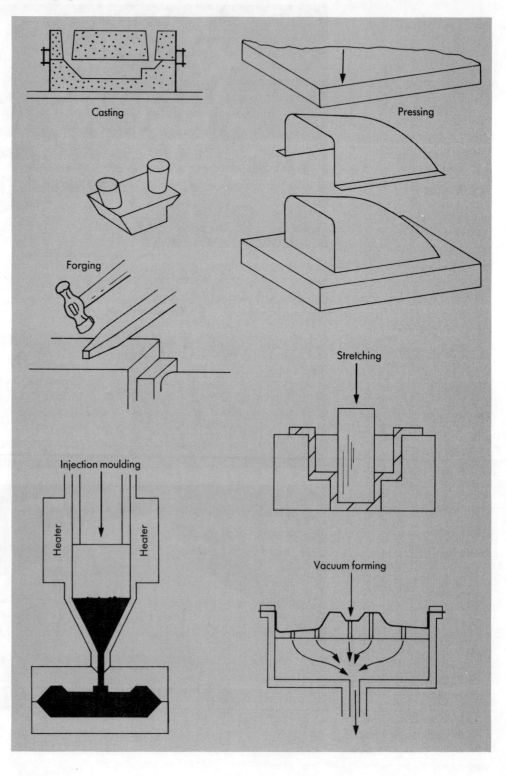

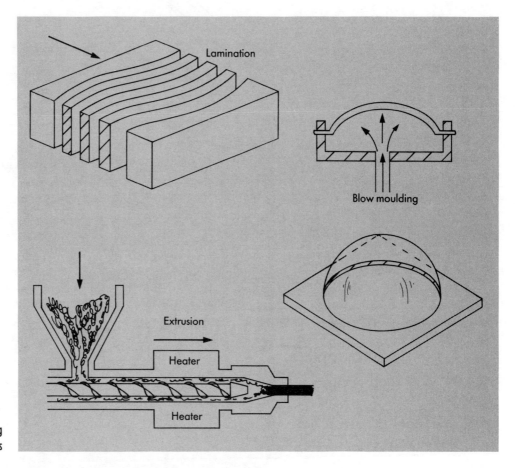

Fig. 6.5 Various rearranging techniques

The **advantages** of rearranging materials are:

- you produce a shape which is structurally strong;
- it is economical in the use of material;
- once you have made a mould you can quickly produce a large number of items.

The **disadvantage** is:

- it is a time consuming and expensive process to produce a mould.

ADDITION

Addition is another forming method.

This is also known as *prefabrication* and is when you make the shape required out of a number of pieces of material, which are joined together. All materials can be formed into a shape by using a variety of fastenings, joints and adhesives to fix the components together. Sometimes (particularly when joining metals or plastics) heat may be used.

Fig. 6.6 outlines a range of techniques you can use for addition.

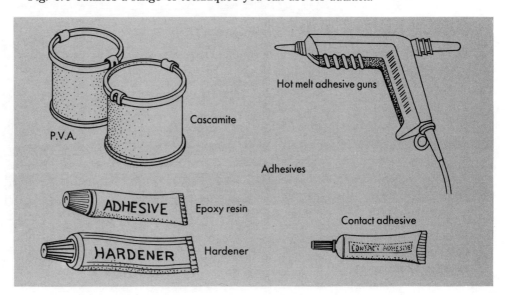

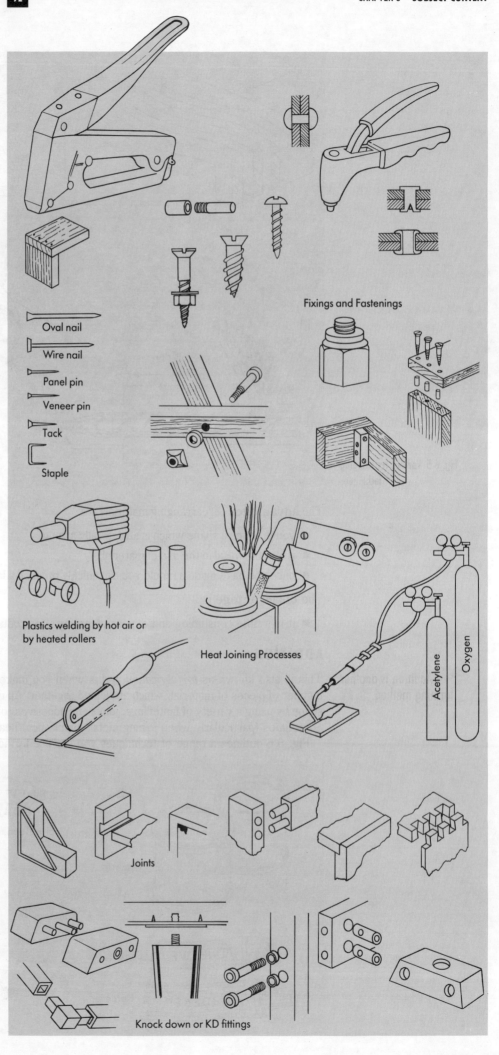

Fixings and Fastenings

Oval nail

Wire nail

Panel pin

Veneer pin

Tack

Staple

Plastics welding by hot air or
by heated rollers

Heat Joining Processes

Acetylene

Oxygen

Joints

Knock down or KD fittings

Fig. 6.6 A range of the techniques
you can use for addition (prefabrication)

The **advantages** of using addition to shape materials are:

- you can quickly produce frame structures;
- you can produce shapes which are difficult to form in any other way;
- you can add to the shape produced, if greater strength is needed;
- you can join different materials together;
- the process is usually economical in the use of materials and time.

The **disadvantages** of using addition to shape materials are:

- the strength of the finished object may be more dependent on the quality of the joints, fastenings or adhesives used than on the material components.

SUBTRACTION

> **Subtraction is a third forming method.**

This is when part of the material is cut away or wasted to get the shape you need. Again this method of forming can be used with all types of material and is sometimes used after a material has been formed by rearranging or addition. For example, castings are often further machined after having been formed in the mould.

In subtraction the materials are shaped by the use of a variety of hand and machine processes or by a combination of both.

Fig. 6.7 outlines a number of hand tool techniques which can be used for subtraction.

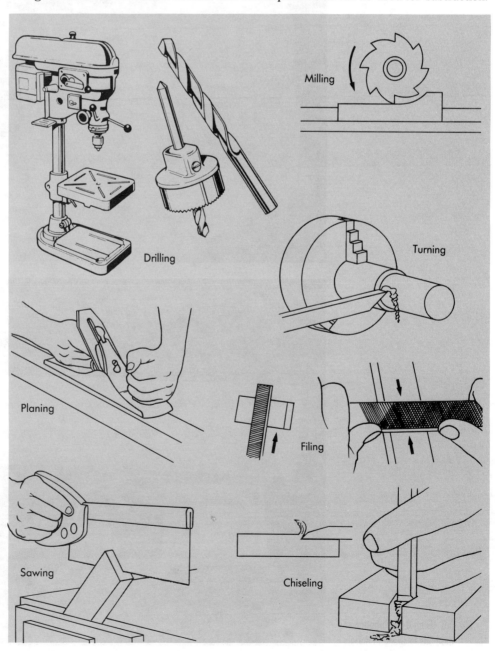

Fig. 6.7 A range of techniques for subtraction

The **advantages** of using subtraction to shape materials are:

- the component is formed from the solid material and is normally structurally sound;
- particularly when machine tools are used a high degree of accuracy can be achieved;

The **disadvantage** of using subtraction to shape materials is:

- you waste part of the material.

> **In practice, a combination of forming methods is often used.**

In practice, most articles are shaped by a **combination** of the three methods.

In the final project examples shown in Fig. 6.8 you can see that all three methods of shaping materials have been used. One project has used *subtraction* for drilling the holes and *re-arranging* to form the box for the electronics. The other project has used *re-arranging* for the control box and *addition* to help form the casing of the tunnel.

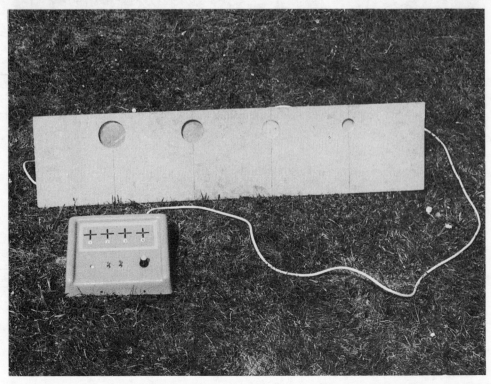

Fig. 6.8 Using a combination of methods to shape materials

2 ▷ WORKING PROPERTIES OF MATERIALS

To use materials successfully you must also know about their *working properties*. This will often be a deciding factor in the choice of material you make for a particular purpose.

Each material will have a range of advantages and disadvantages in each of the following properties:

66 Important working properties of materials. **99**

- Ductility.
- Elasticity.
- Electrical Conductivity.
- Hardness.
- Malleability.
- Resistance to Corrosion.
- Thermal range.
- Toughness.

Fig. 6.9 provides more information on each of these important working properties of materials.

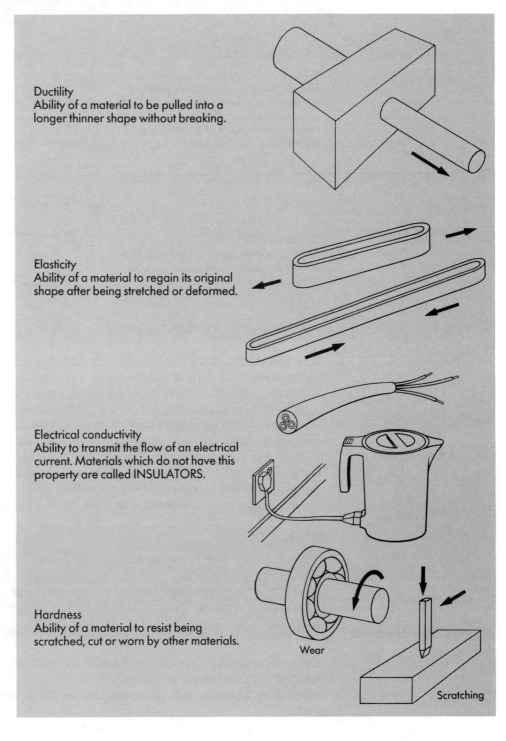

Ductility
Ability of a material to be pulled into a longer thinner shape without breaking.

Elasticity
Ability of a material to regain its original shape after being stretched or deformed.

Electrical conductivity
Ability to transmit the flow of an electrical current. Materials which do not have this property are called INSULATORS.

Hardness
Ability of a material to resist being scratched, cut or worn by other materials.

Wear

Scratching

Fig. 6.9 Outline of working properties of materials

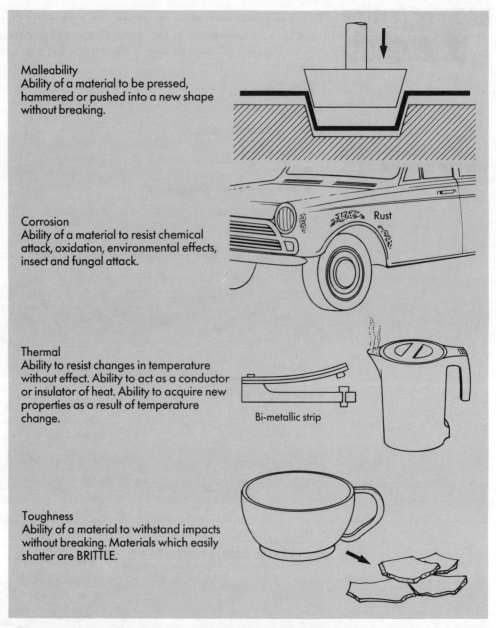

Malleability
Ability of a material to be pressed, hammered or pushed into a new shape without breaking.

Corrosion
Ability of a material to resist chemical attack, oxidation, environmental effects, insect and fungal attack.

Rust

Thermal
Ability to resist changes in temperature without effect. Ability to act as a conductor or insulator of heat. Ability to acquire new properties as a result of temperature change.

Bi-metallic strip

Toughness
Ability of a material to withstand impacts without breaking. Materials which easily shatter are BRITTLE.

It is important to know both advantages **and** disadvantages of a material for each property; sometimes you may wish to make use of a disadvantage as well as an advantage. For example, a suitable material for the body of an electric kettle might need to have **good** properties of thermal insulation and **poor** properties of electrical conductivity.

The materials you use will also have their own individual properties of texture, colour and sometimes smell. These, together with their qualities in terms of our list of properties, will help you to identify an appropriate individual material.

> A materials chart may help.

During your course you will use and gain experience of a wide range of materials; it will be almost impossible to remember every property of all the materials you use. It will, therefore, help to make a *materials chart*, like the one in Fig. 6.10.

WOOD			
Name	Source	Properties	Uses
METALS			
Name	Melting point	Properties	Uses
PLASTICS			
Name	Softening point	Properties	Uses

Fig. 6.10 Materials chart: structure

Keep a record of the materials you regularly use and build up your own chart. The chart below (Fig. 6.11) will give you a start.

Remember, when you talk about materials in any aspect of your course, try to be **specific**.

WOOD

NAME	SOURCE	PROPERTIES	USES
Hardwoods European Oak	Britain and Europe	Very strong and durable. Very stable, ideal for outdoor use when properly finished. Works well with sharp tools. Contains tannic acid which will corrode steel and some other metal fittings, leaving a blue stain. Light to dark brown with some silver streaking in the figure.	Garden furniture, furniture, gates, fence posts, flooring, veneers. Can also be used for boat building and interior fittings. Furniture and general interior work.
Japanese Oak	Japan	Strong and durable although overall weaker than European type. Easily worked and much cheaper than European type. Very good for bending and lamination. Yellowish brown in colour with a fairly plain figure.	All general interior work including flooring and furniture.
Softwoods Redwood Scots Pine	Northern Europe and Scandinavia, Scotland	Fairly strong, being harder than most softwoods, with a straight grain. Easily worked and finishes well. Some boards can be knotty and troublesome to work. Pale reddish brown colour with clear growth ring marking in the figure.	Heavy constructional work, including roof trusses, plywood and all general interior work.
Sitka Spruce Whitewood	Canada, U.S.A., Northern Europe	Strong and easily worked with a straight grain. Can suffer from resin pockets in some boards which may affect paint and other finishes. It is cheap and easily obtained. Almost white in colour with a plain figure.	Interior 'whitewood' furniture and other general uses. Exterior uses include telegraph poles. One of the most used softwoods.
Douglas Fir	Canada, U.S.A.	Fairly soft and easily worked. Straight, knot-free grain. Easily finished. Almost white to reddish brown in colour.	General construction work and plywood.

METALS

NAME	MELTING POINT	PROPERTIES	USES
Ferrous Steels	1400°C	Alloy of iron and carbon. Type defined by the amount of carbon present.	
Low carbon steel		Less than 0.15% carbon. Soft, ductile and malleable. Cannot be hardened.	Used for pressings, wire.
Mild steel		0.15% to 0.30% carbon. Most widely used of all the steels. High tensile strength combined with good ductility and reasonable malleability. Works well and is easily fabricated. Can only be case hardened.	General purpose steel, most used. All types fabrication, screws, nuts and bolts.
High carbon steel		0.7% to 1.4% carbon. Very hard and tough but with poor ductility and malleability. Can be hardened and tempered.	Many types of wood, metal and plastic cutting tools.
High speed steel		Alloy of medium carbon steel and tungsten, chromium and vanadium. Very hard and brittle. Has the ability to retain hardness at very high temperatures. Can be hardened and tempered.	Drills, lathe-cutting tools, milling and router cutters.
Stainless steel		Alloy of steel with chromium and small quantities of nickel. It is tough and very resistant to all types of corrosion. Can be hard to work.	Sink units, cutlery, specialised chemical tanks and piping.

NAME	MELTING POINT	PROPERTIES	USES
Non-Ferrous Aluminium	650°C	Greyish white metal, very light and soft. As a pure metal it is highly ductile and malleable. Very good electrical conductivity and resistance to corrosion. Very easy to work.	Packaging and insulation, electrical conductors. Household goods, saucepans, foil.
Duralumin		Alloy of aluminium and copper with a small amount of manganese. This improves the toughness of the aluminium and produces a strong light metal. This alloy machines very well.	Aircraft and vehicle parts.
Copper	1100°C	A reddish coloured metal which is heavy, ductile and quite strong. It can be easily pressed or beaten into shape. However, it easily work hardens and requires frequent annealing. Very good electrical conductivity and resistance to corrosion.	Electrical wire, piping. Specialised roof coverings.
Brass	980°C	A golden yellow coloured alloy of copper and zinc. Made in a variety of types, depending on the ratio between the copper and zinc in the alloy. Harder than copper it works and casts well. It is a good electrical conductor. Good resistance to corrosion but will tarnish easily.	Taps, valves, gas and water pipe connectors. All types of casting and ornamental uses.

PLASTICS			
NAME	SOFTENING POINT	PROPERTIES	USES
Thermoplastics Acrylic (PMMA)	110°C	Very hard and stiff, available in transparent, translucent and opaque forms. Can be brittle but is much stronger than glass. Not affected by weather and most solvents. Easily worked and can be polished to a high finish. Good electrical insulator and is safe to use with food.	Electrical unit covers, e.g. hi-fi. Lights and illuminated signs. Sinks, baths, shower bases.
Nylon	220°C	Available in many types. One of the most commonly used is nylon 6. Very tough, rigid and resistant to creep. Has the property of being self-lubricating and is resistant to friction and wear. Machines easily but is difficult to join. High melting point.	Bearings, gears, power tool casings. Clothing and fabrics. Household fittings, curtain rails, hinges.
Polypropylene	100°C	Light, floats, very resistant to chemical attack and fatigue. Good impact properties at low temperatures.	Hinges, crates, syringes. Chemical piping.
Polystyrene	85°C	Light, hard and stiff. Can be toughened to produce good impact properties. Easily moulded and is an ideal injection moulding material. Available in a wide variety of colours and is suitable for use with food.	Model kits, food containers, toys, cabinets, refrigerator linings.

Fig. 6.11 Materials chart: sample content

The main type of materials which you will use are *metals, woods* and *plastics*. Whilst you will only need very detailed knowledge about them if you are taking the specialist materials module, you should know about their basic properties and differences (Fig. 6.12) and the forms in which they can be obtained (Fig. 6.13).

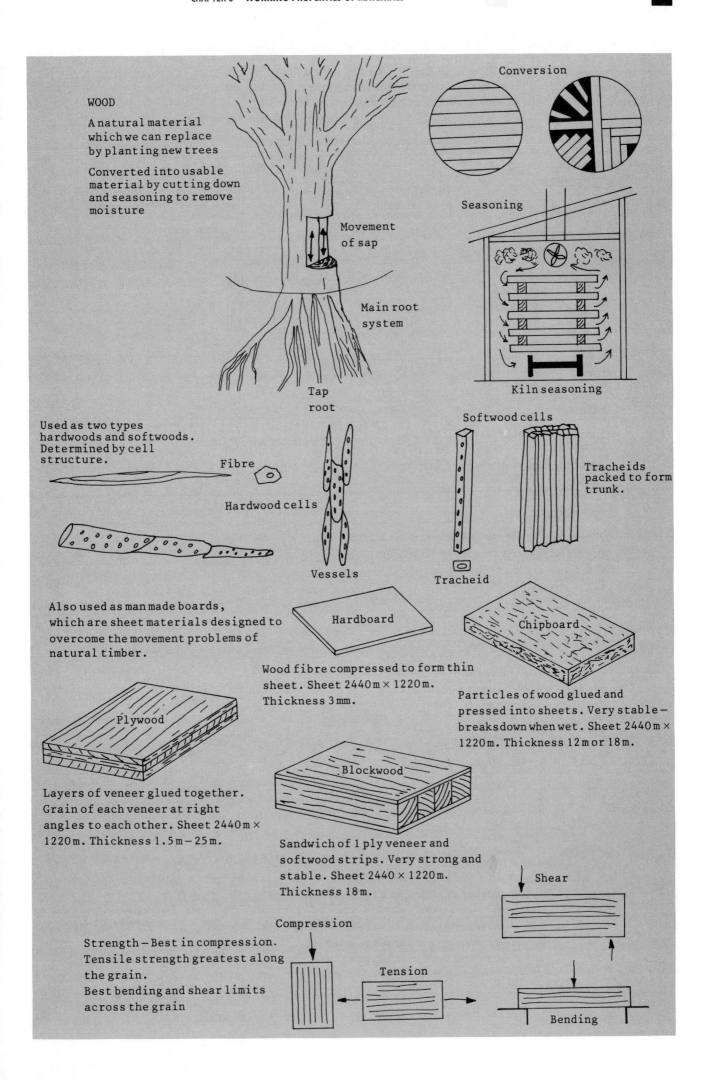

WOOD

A natural material which we can replace by planting new trees

Converted into usable material by cutting down and seasoning to remove moisture

Movement of sap

Main root system

Tap root

Conversion

Seasoning

Kiln seasoning

Used as two types hardwoods and softwoods. Determined by cell structure.

Fibre

Hardwood cells

Vessels

Softwood cells

Tracheids packed to form trunk.

Tracheid

Also used as man made boards, which are sheet materials designed to overcome the movement problems of natural timber.

Hardboard

Wood fibre compressed to form thin sheet. Sheet 2440m × 1220m. Thickness 3mm.

Chipboard

Particles of wood glued and pressed into sheets. Very stable — breaks down when wet. Sheet 2440m × 1220m. Thickness 12m or 18m.

Plywood

Layers of veneer glued together. Grain of each veneer at right angles to each other. Sheet 2440m × 1220m. Thickness 1.5m — 25m.

Blockwood

Sandwich of 1 ply veneer and softwood strips. Very strong and stable. Sheet 2440 × 1220m. Thickness 18m.

Strength — Best in compression. Tensile strength greatest along the grain. Best bending and shear limits across the grain

Compression

Tension

Shear

Bending

METALS

Metals are produced from ores by smelting and then either casting into ingots, rolling, or extruding into usable forms.

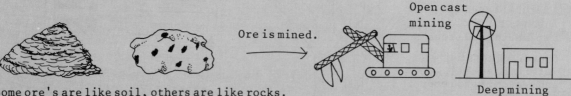

Ore is mined.

Open cast mining

Deep mining

Some ore's are like soil, others are like rocks.

Then smelted into the metal

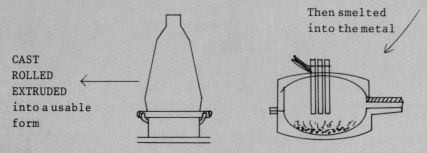

CAST
ROLLED
EXTRUDED
into a usable
form

Metals exist as:

FERROUS

These are the metals containing ferrite or iron. The most common is steel which is a mixture of iron and carbon.

NON-FERROUS

These are the metals which contain no ferrite. The most common is aluminium which is a light grey colour, very light and soft.

ALLOYS

These are mixtures of two or more metals. They are made to improve the properties of the main metal in the mixture or to make a new metal. Alloys can be ferrous or non-ferrous.

e.g. Stainless Steel – Ferrous – steel + chromium + nickel.
Brass – Non-ferrous – copper + zinc.

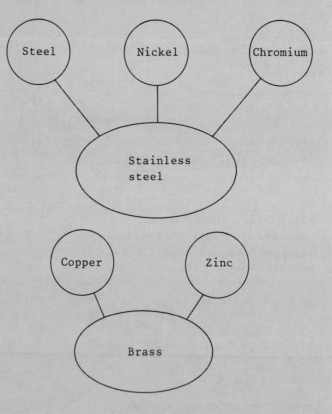

Steel   Nickel   Chromium

Stainless steel

Copper   Zinc

Brass

PLASTICS

Plastics are derived from oil and coal and are processed into powders, granules and resins. They are then re-processed by a variety of techniques into usable forms.

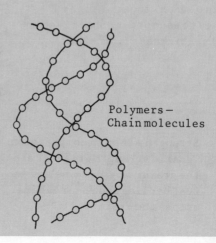

Polymers –
Chain molecules

THERMOSETS

These are plastics which once moulded will always retain their shape. If reheated they will not soften again.

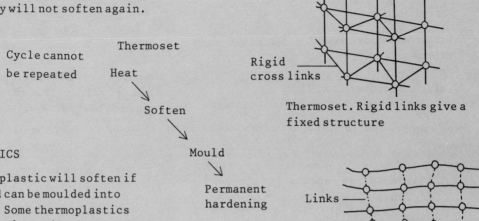

Cycle cannot be repeated

Thermoset

Heat
↘
Soften
↘
Mould
↘
Permanent hardening

Rigid cross links

Thermoset. Rigid links give a fixed structure

THERMOPLASTICS

This type of plastic will soften if reheated and can be moulded into shape again. Some thermoplastics have a 'memory' and will try to go back to their previous shape when reheated.

To form plastics heat must always be present. Either the plastic has to be heated from an external source, e.g. — electric element, or the heat is present as part of a chemical reaction between two resins.

e.g. Epoxy resin — mixture of hardener and resin.
Polyester resin — mixture of resin and catalyst.

Links

Thermoplastic. Weak linking bonds give a flexible structure

Cycle can be repeated

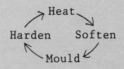

Thermoplastic

Heat
Harden   Soften
Mould

COMPOSITES

Glass Reinforced Plastic is a mixture of polyester resin and glass fibre. By themselves both of these materials are relatively weak. Polyester resin is very brittle. Glass fibre has little strength. However, when they are mixed the glass fibre acts as a reinforcing to the polyester resin and a strong flexible material is produced.

Carbon fibre can also be used as a reinforcing agent with polyester resin or epoxy resin.

Concrete is another example of a composite material. Cement, a weak material by itself, is mixed with water and an aggregate to form a strong, easily moulded material This can be made even stronger by the use of steel rods or reinforcing mesh.

Many of the new ceramic materials being developed are also examples of composites.

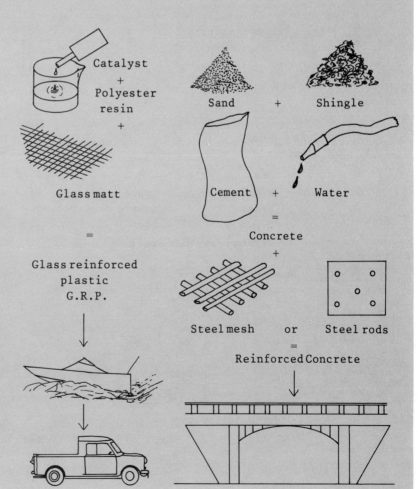

Catalyst + Polyester resin +

Glass matt

=

Glass reinforced plastic G.R.P.

Sand + Shingle

Cement + Water

=

Concrete

+

Steel mesh or Steel rods

=

Reinforced Concrete

Fig. 6.12 Properties of various materials

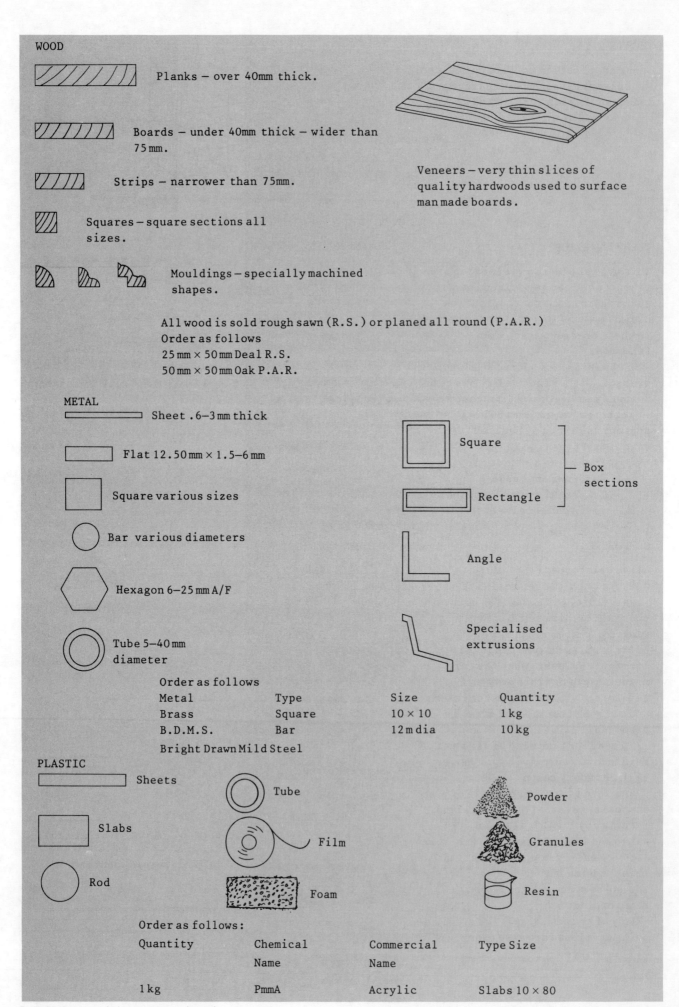

WOOD

Planks — over 40mm thick.

Boards — under 40mm thick — wider than 75mm.

Strips — narrower than 75mm.

Squares — square sections all sizes.

Mouldings — specially machined shapes.

Veneers — very thin slices of quality hardwoods used to surface man made boards.

All wood is sold rough sawn (R.S.) or planed all round (P.A.R.)
Order as follows
25 mm × 50 mm Deal R.S.
50 mm × 50 mm Oak P.A.R.

METAL

Sheet .6–3 mm thick

Flat 12.50 mm × 1.5–6 mm

Square various sizes

Bar various diameters

Hexagon 6–25 mm A/F

Tube 5–40 mm diameter

Square — Box sections

Rectangle — Box sections

Angle

Specialised extrusions

Order as follows

Metal	Type	Size	Quantity
Brass	Square	10 × 10	1 kg
B.D.M.S.	Bar	12 m dia	10 kg

Bright Drawn Mild Steel

PLASTIC

Sheets

Slabs

Rod

Tube

Film

Foam

Powder

Granules

Resin

Order as follows:

Quantity	Chemical Name	Commercial Name	Type Size
1 kg	PmmA	Acrylic	Slabs 10 × 80

Fig. 6.13 Forms in which materials are obtained

3 > FORCES

When we use materials in any structure they must be able to resist a range of internal and external *forces*.

The forces which may act upon the structures are:

- Tension.
- Compression.
- Shear.
- Bending.
- Torsion.

66 Important forces. 99

In Fig. 6.14 we look at these forces in rather more detail.

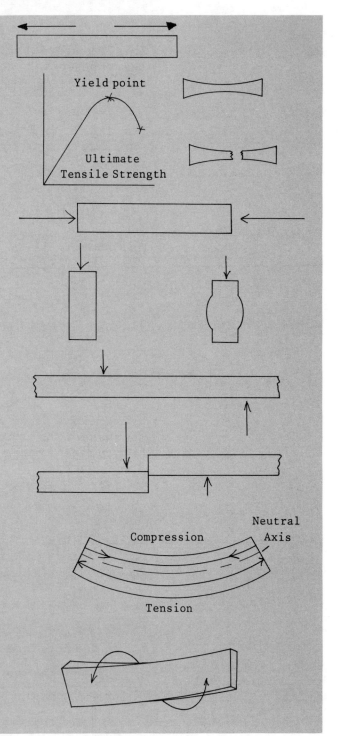

TENSION

The ability of the material to resist being pulled apart. The maximum load the material can withstand without change, is known as its TENSILE STRENGTH.

COMPRESSION

The ability of the material to resist being squashed. The maximum load the material can withstand without change, is known as its COMPRESSIVE STRENGTH.

SHEAR

The ability of the material to resist different parts of it being pushed in opposite directions. The maximum load the material can withstand without change, is known as its SHEAR LIMIT.

BENDING

The ability of the material to resist a static, not moving, load or a dynamic, moving, load. The maximum the material can withstand without change, is known as its BENDING LIMIT.

TORSION

The ability of a material to resist a turning action or torque applied to it.

Fig. 6.14 The various types of force

For the structure to retain its shape both the external and internal forces must be equal, and the structure is said to be in *equilibrium*. It is also important to use a safety factor when designing a structure. You should make sure that the materials are not being used to the limit of their properties.

USE OF SHAPE TO RESIST FORCES

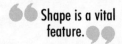

When materials are used in a structure, the *shape* of the *individual components* or the overall shape of the *structure* is designed to resist the forces acting upon it. Fig. 6.15 looks at examples of how this is achieved.

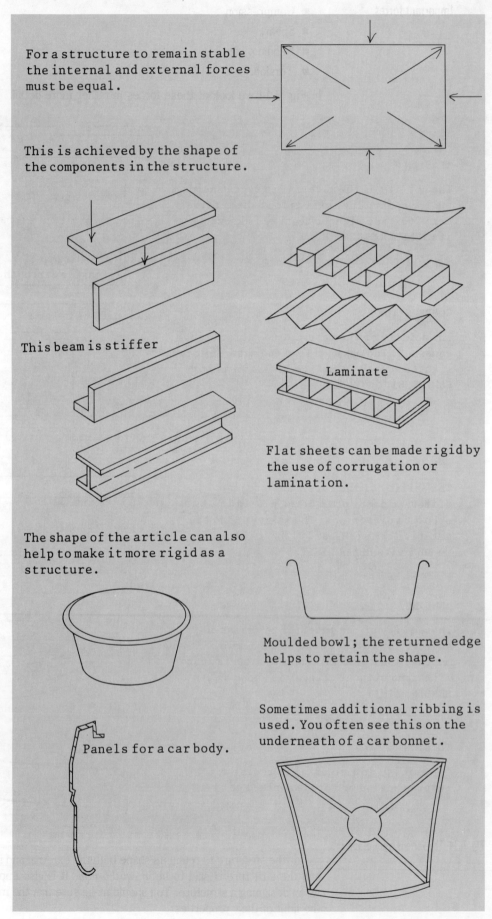

For a structure to remain stable the internal and external forces must be equal.

This is achieved by the shape of the components in the structure.

This beam is stiffer

Laminate

Flat sheets can be made rigid by the use of corrugation or lamination.

The shape of the article can also help to make it more rigid as a structure.

Moulded bowl; the returned edge helps to retain the shape.

Panels for a car body.

Sometimes additional ribbing is used. You often see this on the underneath of a car bonnet.

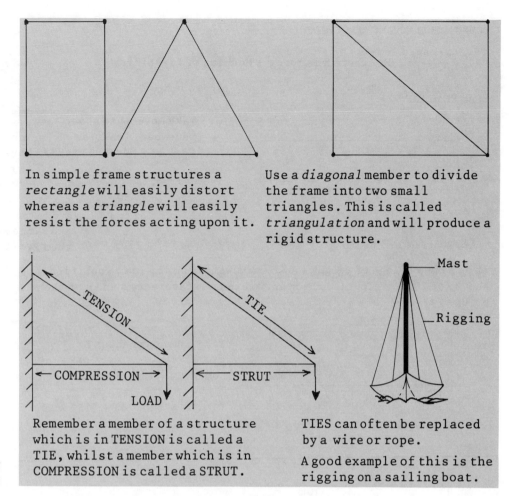

In simple frame structures a *rectangle* will easily distort whereas a *triangle* will easily resist the forces acting upon it.

Use a *diagonal* member to divide the frame into two small triangles. This is called *triangulation* and will produce a rigid structure.

Remember a member of a structure which is in TENSION is called a TIE, whilst a member which is in COMPRESSION is called a STRUT.

TIES can often be replaced by a wire or rope.

A good example of this is the rigging on a sailing boat.

Fig. 6.15 Using shape to resist forces

USE OF EQUATIONS AND CALCULATIONS

When you apply your material and structural knowledge to a problem you may have to make use of *calculations* to help you find a solution or to see if the material you have chosen or the structure you have designed is suitable or safe. Fig. 6.16 provides examples of the equations and calculations you need to be familiar with.

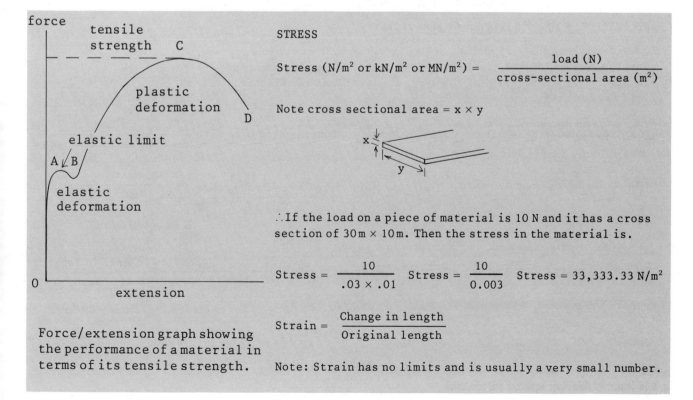

STRESS

$$\text{Stress (N/m}^2 \text{ or kN/m}^2 \text{ or MN/m}^2) = \frac{\text{load (N)}}{\text{cross-sectional area (m}^2)}$$

Note cross sectional area = x × y

∴ If the load on a piece of material is 10 N and it has a cross section of 30 m × 10 m. Then the stress in the material is.

$$\text{Stress} = \frac{10}{.03 \times .01} \quad \text{Stress} = \frac{10}{0.003} \quad \text{Stress} = 33,333.33 \text{ N/m}^2$$

$$\text{Strain} = \frac{\text{Change in length}}{\text{Original length}}$$

Note: Strain has no limits and is usually a very small number.

Force/extension graph showing the performance of a material in terms of its tensile strength.

YOUNG'S MODULUS OF ELASTICITY

$$\frac{stress}{strain} = E. \text{ (where E is Young's Modulus of Elasticity}$$

BEAM REACTIONS

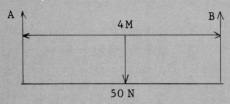

Take movements about A
Remember Clockwise   = Anticlockwise
                Movements (CM)   Movements (ACM)

$$50 \times 2 = R_B \times 4$$

$$R_B = \frac{50 \times 2}{4}$$

$$R_B = 25 \text{ N} \qquad \text{and since } R_A + R_B = 50 \text{ N}$$
$$\text{then } R_A = 50 \text{ N}$$

If we have a bridge of weight 150 kN and a weight on it, in the position shown, of 20 kN, calculate the reaction in the statements A and B of the bridge.

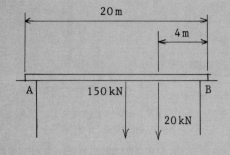

Take movements about B

Sum of CM = sum of ACM

$$R_A \times 20 = (20 \times 4) + (150 \times 10)$$

$$20 R_A = 80 + 1500$$

$$20 R_A = 1580$$

$$R_A = 79 \text{ kN}$$

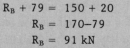

It can now be seen that
$$R_B + 79 = 150 + 20$$
$$R_B = 170 - 79$$
$$R_B = 91 \text{ kN}$$

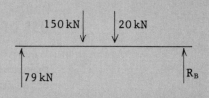

APPLICATION OF YOUNG'S MODULUS OF ELASTICITY

If a wire 3 m long and 4.25 mm diameter is extended by 0.8 mm when a tensile force of 200 N is applied to it, calculate Young's modulus of elasticity for the material of the wire, assuming that the elastic limit has not been exceeded.

Cross-sectional area of wire $= \frac{\pi}{4} \times (4.25)^2 \text{ mm}^2$

$$= 14.19 \text{ mm}^2$$

Tensile stress in wire $= \dfrac{load}{cross\text{-}sectional\ area}$

$$= \frac{200 \text{ N}}{14.19 \text{ mm}^2}$$

$$= 14.09 \text{ N/mm}^2$$

Original length of wire = 3 m (3000 mm)

Extension of wire = 0.8 mm

Tensile strain in wire $= \dfrac{extension\ (change\ in\ length)}{original\ length}$

$$= \frac{0.8}{3000}$$

$$= 0.00027$$

Fig. 6.16 Important definitions, equations and calculations

SAMPLE QUESTIONS AND RESPONSES

QUESTIONS INVOLVING MATERIAL AND STRUCTURAL KNOWLEDGE

The following are examples of questions from the written examination which are testing your material and structural knowledge. There are further examples in Chapter 3.

Questions with outline answers

This group of questions requires you to make use of your basic structures and materials knowledge.

Question 1

In the diagrams below you are shown a kitchen storage unit.

a) On Fig. 6.17 clearly show which surface of the shelf is in compression and which is in tension. *(2)*

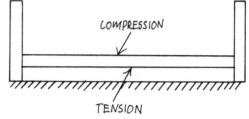

Fig. 6.17

b) If the shelf is loaded, as shown in Fig. 6.18,

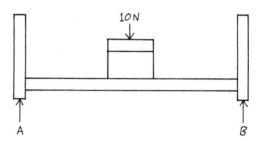

Fig. 6.18

   i) what is the reaction in the members A and B?

   A = 5N   B = 5 N

   _____

   ii) what type of force is acting in the members A and B?

   Compression

   _____ *(4)*
   (ULEAC)

Question 2

In Fig. 6.19 you are shown a stainless steel sink and a polythene washing up bowl. Both of these articles are formed from sheet materials.

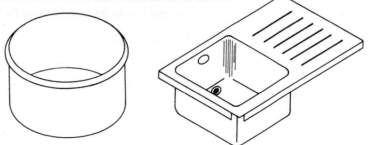

Fig. 6.19

---

a) i) With notes and sketches explain how either the sink or the washing up bowl are formed.

Produce a mould of the bowl.

Heating element

1 Mould placed in vacuum former.

2 Plastic sheet heated.

3 Air removed.

Heating element

4 Air pressure pushes plastic over mould to form bowl.

Plate is raised/air removed
bowl formed

ii) Name the forming process used for the article you have described.

    Vacuum forming   (8)

b) Explain how the sink or washing up bowl remains rigid after forming.

    The returned edges and shape of the bowl help to retain
    its shape and make it rigid. Also, as the thermoplastic
    cools its structure becomes rigid again.   (4)
                                                                           (ULEAC)

Practice questions

1   a) Aluminium and steel are two metals which are widely used in industry.

    i) Explain why aluminium is more expensive to produce than steel.

    _____ (2)

    ii) Steel is more likely to corrode than aluminium and is more dense, yet is often
        preferred to aluminium for manufacturing car bodies. Give **two** reasons for this.

        1 _____

        2 _____ (4)

    b) i) Explain, with the help of a simple line drawing, the extrusion process.

                                                                                (6)

ii) Name **one** example of a product that could be made from extruded metal.

_____ (2)

iii) Name **one** product that could be made from extruded plastics.

_____ (2)

c) i) Explain what is meant by an alloy.

_____

_____ (2)

ii) Give **two** examples of alloys. For **each** example give its components.

Alloy 1 _____

Components _____

Alloy 2 _____

Components _____ (8)

(ULEAC)

2 a) Use simple sketches to show **one** method of improving the rigidity of sheet steel.

(4)

b) Explain, with the aid of sketches, how **two** of the following materials may be strengthened.
  i) concrete;
  ii) wood;
  iii) polyester resin.

(10)

A FINAL STATEMENT

- A knowledge of materials and structures is very important.
- You will use this knowledge in all aspects of your CDT: Technology course.
- Keep a note of the properties of the materials you regularly use.
- Try to design your solutions within the limits of the materials' properties.
- Design your structures so that they can resist the forces which will act upon them.
- Remember, the choice of the materials to use for a particular purpose will depend upon the relationship between the following factors:

   COST – PROPERTIES REQUIRED – METHOD OF MANUFACTURE

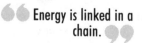

4 ⟩ **ENERGY**

❝ Energy is linked in a chain. ❞

Energy is very important to us, we use it all the time. For example when you work or play sport you use energy. Your energy comes from the food you eat. You have converted the energy you obtained by eating, into movement to do your work or play sport. This is called an _energy chain_. Two different types are illustrated in Fig. 6.20.

At each stage in the chain the energy is converted from one form to another, but it is not destroyed. This shows us a very important principle:

- Energy cannot be destroyed or created, only converted into another form.

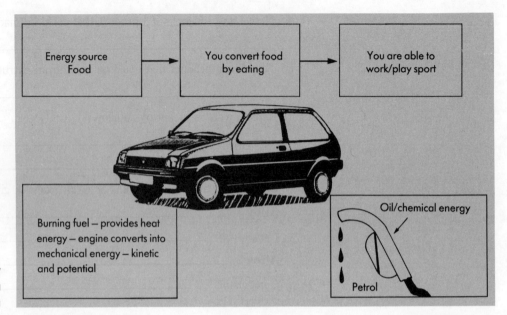

Fig. 6.20 Examples of energy chains or energy conversions into a useful form

ENERGY EFFICIENCY

However, whenever we convert energy from one form to another a little is 'lost'; this is because no method of energy conversion is 100% efficient. For example, when the engine of a car converts the chemical energy contained in petrol into mechanical energy causing the car to move, some of the energy appears to be 'lost'. This is because friction has changed some of the energy into heat which is absorbed by the metal of the engine or lost to the air. Many of the ways we convert energy are not very efficient. Remember, the more conversions there are in an energy chain, the greater is the amount of 'lost' energy.

❝ Consider energy efficiency. ❞

This is very important. When you design solutions to problems, try to make them as *energy efficient* as possible. For example, industry is becoming increasingly aware of the costs of energy in producing a product, from the raw material to the finished article. Often manufacturers will carry out an energy audit of a *design* to help determine the most energy efficient means of production, or an energy audit of the *factory* to see if the overall energy costs can be reduced. Remember, some materials require very high amounts of energy to produce or form them. Most plastics and metals are high energy cost materials.

Wherever possible, manufacturers try to produce articles which are energy efficient and low in overall production energy costs.

FORMS OF ENERGY

❝ Eight forms of energy. ❞

There are **eight forms** of energy which we use:

- Potential.
- Kinetic.
- Chemical.
- Heat.
- Electrical.
- Light.
- Sound.
- Nuclear.

Fig. 6.21 outlines some of these energy types.

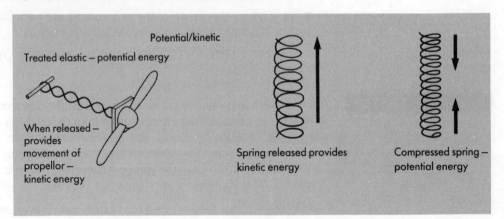

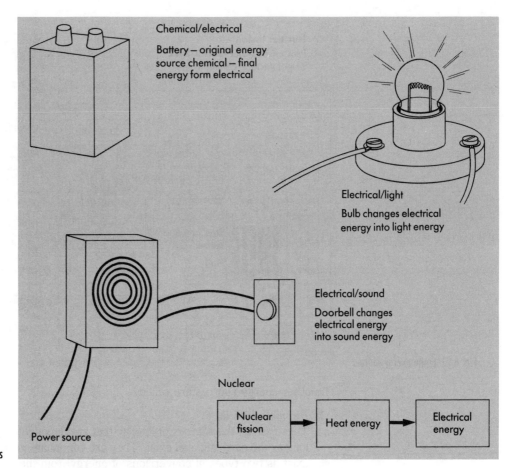

Fig. 6.21 Some energy types

MACHINES AND ENERGY CONVERSION

We use *machines* to convert one form of energy into another, more useful, form.
The sources of the energy we use fall into **two types**.

> ❝ Finite energy sources. ❞

- *Capital – Finite*
  These sources are limited and will eventually run out. Once they have been used they cannot be replaced.
  - Fossil fuels.
  - Coal – oil – natural gas.
  - Nuclear energy.

They are shown in Fig. 6.22.

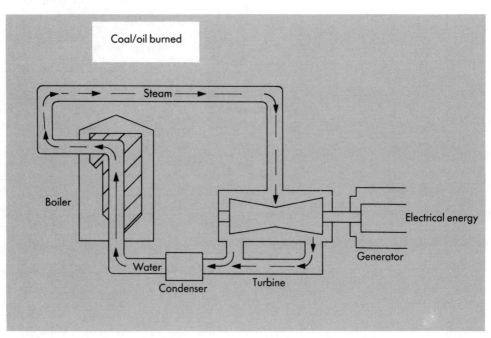

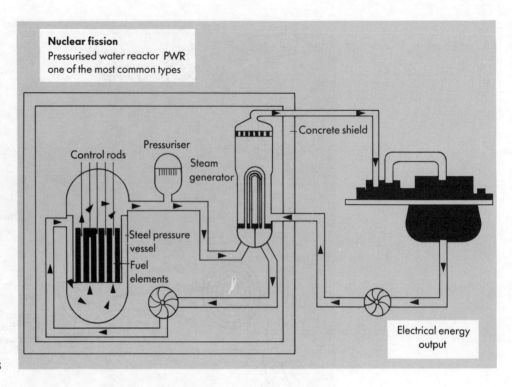

Fig. 6.22 Finite energy sources

The other energy sources are called

- *Income – Infinite*

  These are all the sources of energy that are dependent upon the sun and will last as long as the earth and sun exist. They are continually renewed as we use them. They exist as two types of conversions of energy from the sun (solar radiation).

- *Direct conversion*
  - Solar panels – Solar cells – Solar furnaces

- *Indirect conversions*
  - Wind – Waves – Water – Photosynthesis

Methods of conversion are shown in Fig. 6.23.

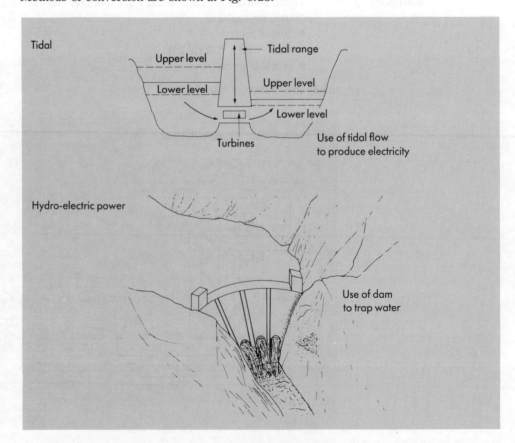

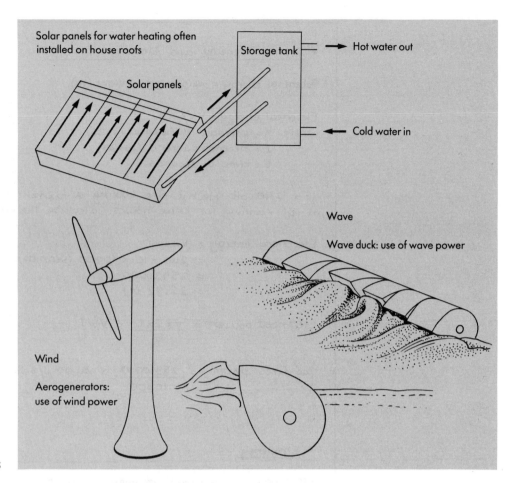

Fig. 6.23 Infinite energy sources

ENERGY CALCULATIONS

Having looked at the forms in which we use energy and the sources from which they are obtained, we now look at how you can *measure* its use. The following are examples of the equations and calculations you need to be familiar with (Fig. 6.24).

• Work and power

Work = force × distance moved
It is measured in Joules

If a load of 5 tonne is raised through a vertical distance of 15m in 30 seconds by a crane. Calculate the work done and the power of the motor.

Work done = force × distance moved.
        = 5000 × 9·81 (N) × 15 (m)
        = 735 750 Nm
        = 735·75 KJ.

Power   = work done   = 735·75 KJ
           time taken   30 seconds

        = 24·52 KJ/s
        = 24·52 KW

Work done in lifting load = 735·5 KJ
Power of crane motor   = 24·52 KW

Power is also   energy transferred (joules)
              time taken to transfer the energy (seconds)

• Potential energy and Electrical energy

Potential energy = weight (N) x height (m)

Electrical energy = V x I x t
where V = potential difference (volts)
      I = electric current (amps)
      t = time in seconds

If a 240 volt electric fire taking a current of 10 amps
is left running for three hours. Calculate the energy used.

Electrical energy = V x I x t
                  = 240 x 10 x 10800 (seconds)
                  = 25920000
                  = 25.92 MJ.

Electrical power = $\dfrac{V \times I \times t}{t}$ = V x I

The fire's power = $\dfrac{25920000}{10800}$ = 2400 J/s = 2400 watts or 2.4 KW.

• Efficiency

Efficiency = $\dfrac{\text{useful works or energy output}}{\text{work or energy input}}$ x 100%

If a hoist is used to lift an engine weighing 400N through 2 metres
The work done = 4000N x 2m = 8000J

In order to do this an effort of 2000N is used and the
hoist operated moves the chain through 20 metres.
The effort moves 20m.

Work done = 2000N x 20m = 40000J

This is the work input of the machine

Efficiency = $\dfrac{\text{output}}{\text{input}}$ x 100% = $\dfrac{8000}{40000}$ x 100 = 20%

Fig. 6.24 Types of energy calculation

The following is a practice question from the written examination which is testing your *energy* knowledge. There are further examples in Chapter 4.

Practice question

The hydraulic hoist of a fork lift truck can load four palettes of soft drinks onto a lorry platform in one minute. If each palette weighs 1000 N and has to be lifted through 1.5 m to the lorry platform, calculate the power of the fork lift's hoist.

Show your working here.

Power of hoist = ——————————   (4)

                                                                          (*Total 11 marks*)
                                                                                    (ULEAC)

A FINAL STATEMENT

- Energy is something you use all the time.
- Energy can never be destroyed or created, only changed from one form to another.
- As a society we are very energy dependent.
- Your use of energy must be as efficient as possible.
- Energy conservation is now very important.

5 > CONTROL SYSTEMS – MECHANICAL AND ELECTRICAL

Most of the objects which are made, and the projects you undertake, will have some form of mechanical or electrical *control* within them. Often they will have a combination of a variety of control systems; for example, many of the mechanical systems of a car are monitored and controlled by electrical and electronic systems.

This part of the book will give you a practical understanding of simple mechanisms, electrical and electronic circuits. The knowledge you gain will be useful in solving problems in your coursework and written papers. If you also study one of the specialist modules in mechanisms, electronics, digital microelectronics or pneumatics, you will have a far deeper control knowledge.

66 A system approach can help. 99

The first thing to remember is that this area is about solving practical problems. The best way of being able to apply your knowledge of mechanisms and electronics is to use a *systems approach* to solving problems. This means that you treat the problem as a 'black box' with an input and an output. In Fig. 6.25 you are shown some examples.

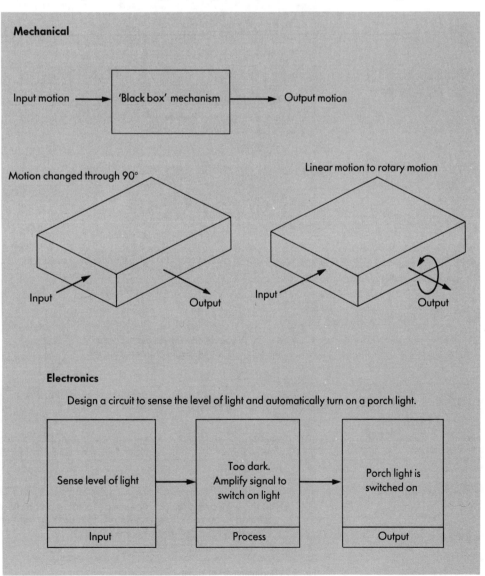

Mechanical

Input motion ⟶ 'Black box' mechanism ⟶ Output motion

Motion changed through 90°

Input

Output

Linear motion to rotary motion

Input

Output

Electronics

Design a circuit to sense the level of light and automatically turn on a porch light.

Sense level of light	Too dark. Amplify signal to switch on light	Porch light is switched on
Input	Process	Output

Fig. 6.25 Systems approach to a problem

If you follow this approach you can remember your mechanisms and electronics as simple building blocks for a particular job. In Fig. 6.26 you are shown a simple 'Darlington driver' circuit. Just by changing the input sensor we can use it to solve a range of problems.

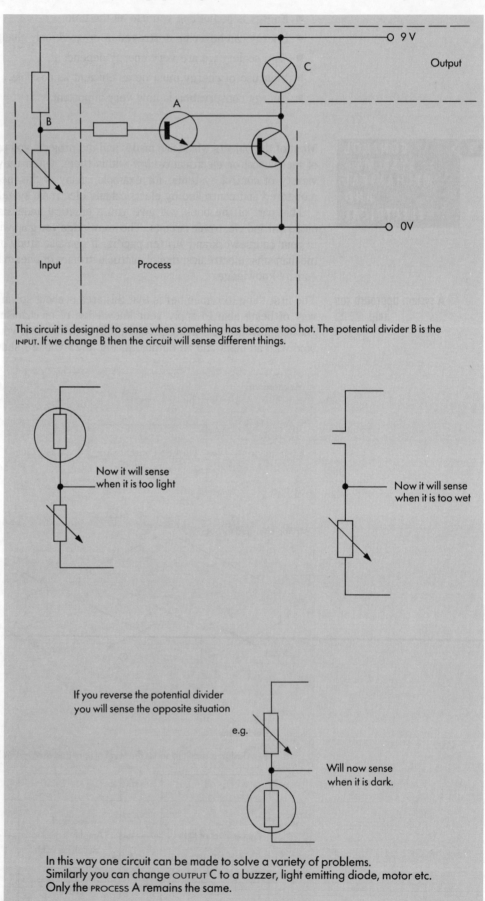

This circuit is designed to sense when something has become too hot. The potential divider B is the INPUT. If we change B then the circuit will sense different things.

Now it will sense when it is too light

Now it will sense when it is too wet

If you reverse the potential divider you will sense the opposite situation

e.g.

Will now sense when it is dark.

In this way one circuit can be made to solve a variety of problems.
Similarly you can change OUTPUT C to a buzzer, light emitting diode, motor etc.
Only the PROCESS A remains the same.

Fig. 6.26 Darlington driver circuit

For example if we:

- use a *photo-cell*, we can sense a change in light level.
- use a *thermistor*, we can sense a change in temperature.
- use a *moisture sensor*, we can sense when it is dry.

By reversing the position of the variable resistor and the sensor we can sense the **opposite** of each situation. By these simple modifications this one building block can solve a whole range of problems.

MOTION

We can achieve the same situation with **mechanical systems**. All mechanical systems will make use of four types of *motion*.

66 Types of motion. **99**

- Linear.
- Rotary.
- Reciprocating.
- Oscillating.

See Fig. 6.27.

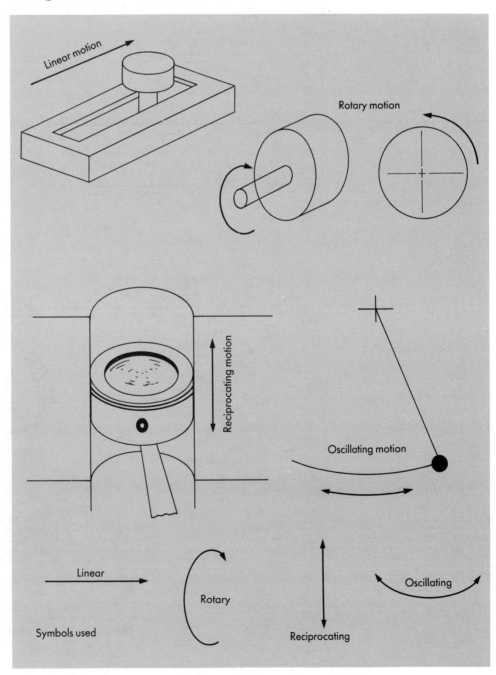

Fig. 6.27 The various types of motion

Sometimes the mechanism is used to **change** the motion. This can be done in a variety of ways:

- Linear into rotary, or vice versa.

- The mechanism can also be used to change the *direction* of motion, from clockwise to anti-clockwise or through 90°.

- It can be used to increase or reduce the *rotational speed* of the output of the system.

See Fig. 6.28.

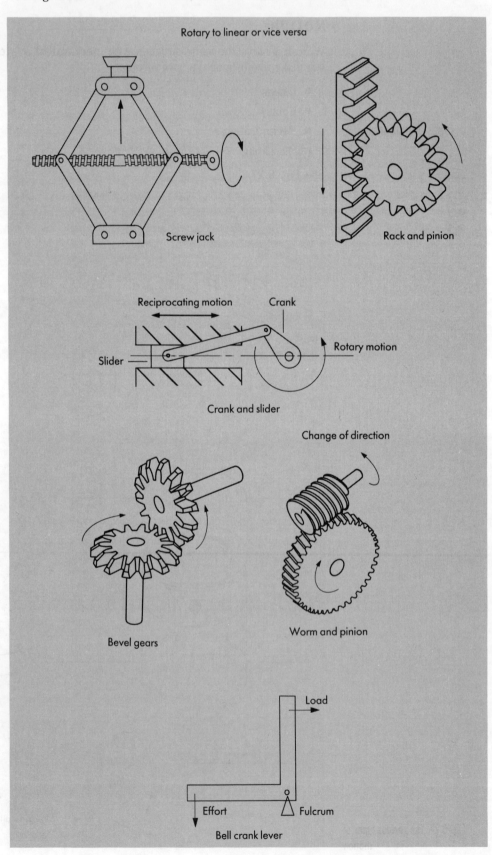

Rotary to linear or vice versa

Screw jack

Rack and pinion

Reciprocating motion   Crank

Slider

Rotary motion

Crank and slider

Change of direction

Bevel gears

Worm and pinion

Load

Effort   Fulcrum

Bell crank lever

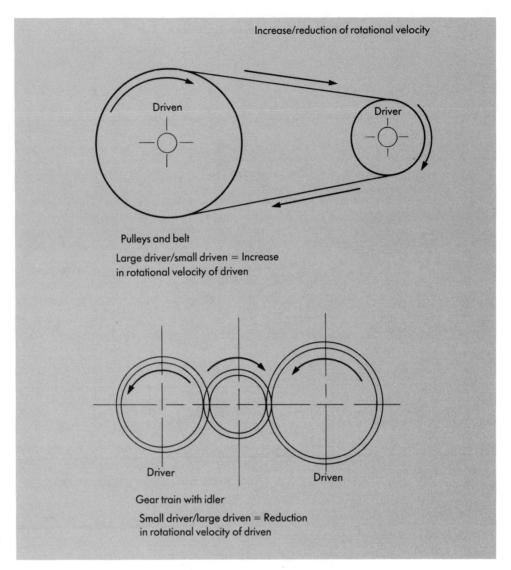

Increase/reduction of rotational velocity

Driven

Driver

Pulleys and belt

Large driver/small driven = Increase
in rotational velocity of driven

Driver

Driven

Gear train with idler

Small driver/large driven = Reduction
in rotational velocity of driven

Fig. 6.28 Using mechanisms to
change motion

Again, if you use a systems approach, certain **rules** can be established which will help you to identify the building blocks to use for a particular problem. It is helpful to make a note of the rules in a simple table, like the one in Fig. 6.29.

TYPE OF MECHANISM	TYPE OF MOTION CHANGE
Rack and pinion	Rotary to linear or linear to rotary
Worm and pinion	Rotary to rotary through 90°. Large reduction.

Fig. 6.29 Making a table of 'rules'

TYPES OF MECHANISM

The mechanisms which you will need to be familiar with can be looked at in four groups.

 **Types of mechanism.**

- Levers and Linkages.
- Pulley systems.
- Gear systems.
- Cams, Eccentrics and Ratchets.

Remember mechanisms are all around you; keep your eyes open and do not take them for granted. As you learn about mechanisms it often helps to use a kit system like LEGO TECHNIC or FISCHER TECKNIC to help to model your ideas. You may already use one as part of your course at school. The best way to revise your knowledge of mechanisms is through practical use.

In Fig. 6.30 you are shown examples of the many different types of mechanism and how they can be used.

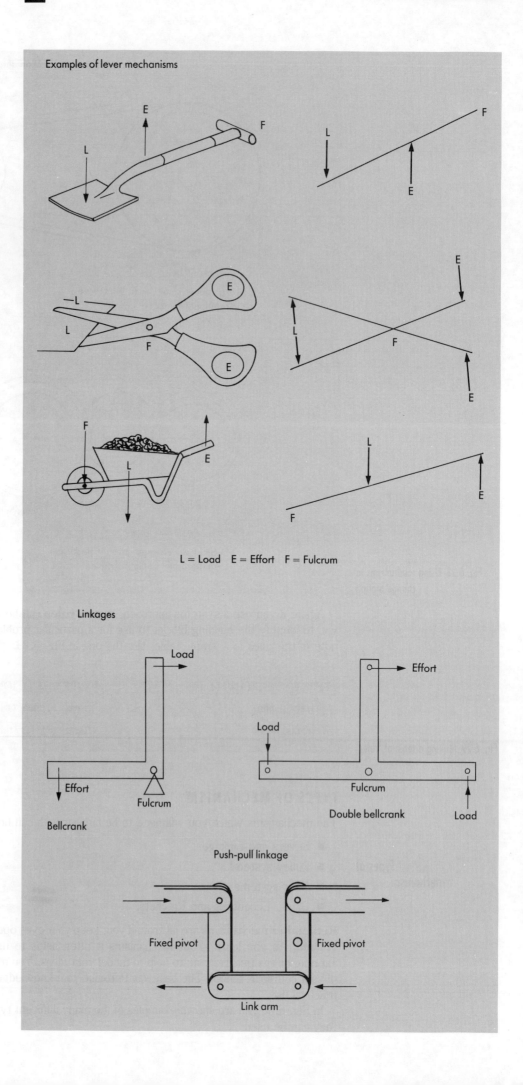

Examples of lever mechanisms

L = Load   E = Effort   F = Fulcrum

Linkages

Load

Effort

Load

Fulcrum

Bellcrank

Effort

Fulcrum

Double bellcrank

Load

Push-pull linkage

Fixed pivot

Fixed pivot

Link arm

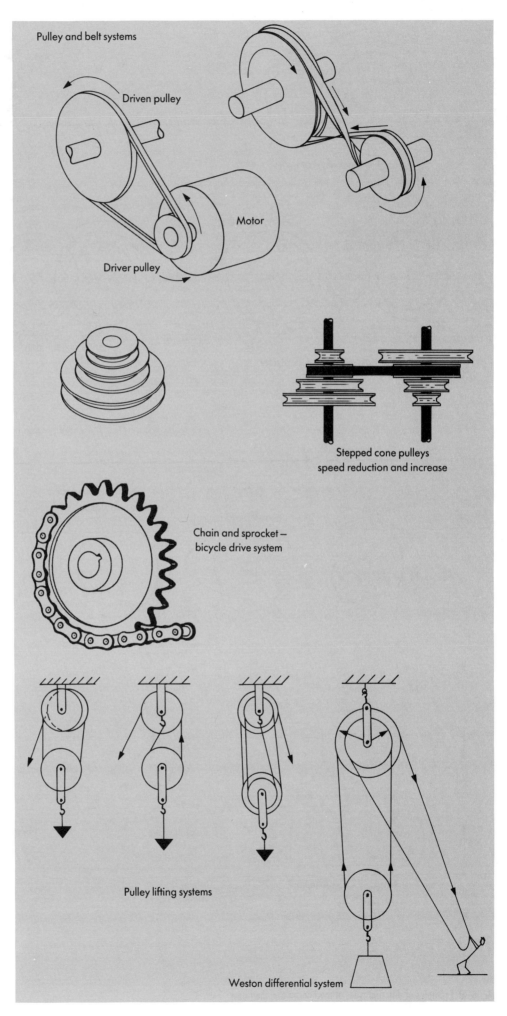

Pulley and belt systems

Driven pulley

Motor

Driver pulley

Stepped cone pulleys
speed reduction and increase

Chain and sprocket –
bicycle drive system

Pulley lifting systems

Weston differential system

Fig. 6.30

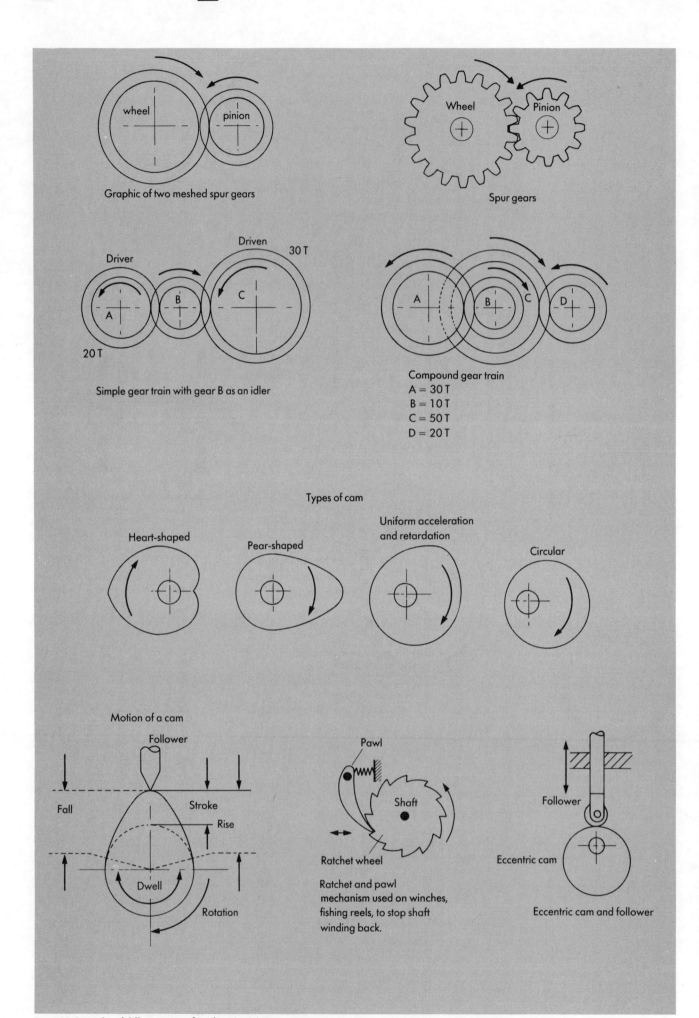

Graphic of two meshed spur gears

Spur gears

Simple gear train with gear B as an idler

Compound gear train
A = 30 T
B = 10 T
C = 50 T
D = 20 T

Types of cam

Heart-shaped

Pear-shaped

Uniform acceleration and retardation

Circular

Motion of a cam

Ratchet and pawl mechanism used on winches, fishing reels, to stop shaft winding back.

Eccentric cam and follower

Fig. 6.30 Examples of different types of mechanism and their uses

EQUATIONS AND CALCULATIONS

In Fig. 6.31, below, are examples of the mechanical equations and calculations you need to be familiar with.

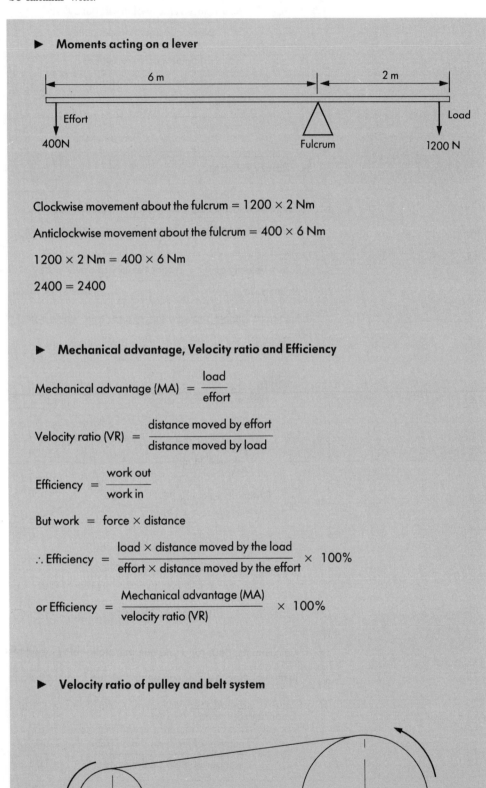

▶ **Moments acting on a lever**

Clockwise movement about the fulcrum = 1200×2 Nm

Anticlockwise movement about the fulcrum = 400×6 Nm

1200×2 Nm = 400×6 Nm

$2400 = 2400$

▶ **Mechanical advantage, Velocity ratio and Efficiency**

$$\text{Mechanical advantage (MA)} = \frac{\text{load}}{\text{effort}}$$

$$\text{Velocity ratio (VR)} = \frac{\text{distance moved by effort}}{\text{distance moved by load}}$$

$$\text{Efficiency} = \frac{\text{work out}}{\text{work in}}$$

But work = force × distance

$$\therefore \text{Efficiency} = \frac{\text{load} \times \text{distance moved by the load}}{\text{effort} \times \text{distance moved by the effort}} \times 100\%$$

$$\text{or Efficiency} = \frac{\text{Mechanical advantage (MA)}}{\text{velocity ratio (VR)}} \times 100\%$$

▶ **Velocity ratio of pulley and belt system**

$$\text{Velocity ratio} = \frac{\text{distance moved by driver pulley}}{\text{distance moved by driven pulley}}$$

$$= \frac{\text{rotary velocity of driver pulley}}{\text{rotary velocity of driven pulley}}$$

$$= \frac{\text{diameter of driven pulley}}{\text{diameter of driver pulley}}$$

▶ **Rotary velocity**

Pulley shaft velocities are calculated from the formula:

rotary velocity of driven pulley × diameter of driven pulley = rotary velocity of driver pulley × diameter of driver pulley

$$\therefore \text{Rotary velocity of driven pulley} = \frac{\text{rotary velocity of driver pulley} \times \text{diameter of driver pulley}}{\text{diameter of driven pulley}}$$

In the figure you are shown a simple gear train which is part of the drive mechanism in a child's toy.

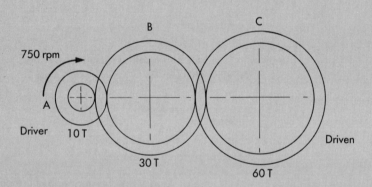

Simple gear train with an idler gear.

Calculate the gear ratio and output (rotational velocity) of the system.

In this situation the idler can be discounted from the calculation.

Gear ratio between C and A

$$= \frac{\text{number of teeth on driven gear}}{\text{number of teeth on driver gear}} = \frac{60}{10} = \frac{6}{1}$$

∴ The gear ratio is 6:1

Rotational velocity of gear C

$$= \frac{\text{velocity of driver gear} \times \text{number of teeth on driver gear}}{\text{number of teeth on driven gear}} = \frac{750 \times 10}{60}$$

$$= 125/\text{revs/min}$$

Fig. 6.31 Mechanical equations and calculations

S A M P L E   Q U E S T I O N S
A N D   R E S P O N S E S

QUESTIONS INVOLVING MECHANICAL KNOWLEDGE

The following are example questions from the written examination which are testing your mechanical knowledge. There are further examples in Chapter 4.

Question 1 and student answer

In Fig. 6.32 you are shown a photograph and black box diagram of the drive mechanism of a food processor.

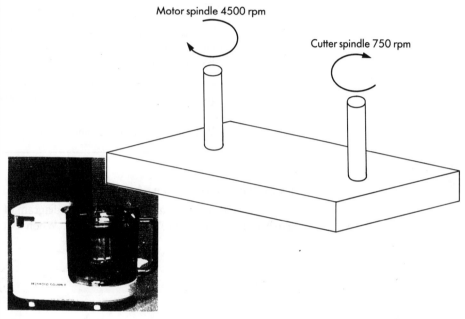

Fig. 6.32

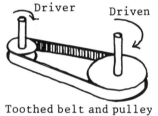

Driver   Driven

Toothed belt and pulley drive

Fig. 6.33 Student answer to 1 a)

a) Sketch a suitable drive mechanism for the food processor. (6)

b) If the spindle speed of the motor is 4500 rpm and the speed of the cutting blades is 750 rpm,

   i) What is the gear or pulley ratio of the system?
   _6 : 1_

   ii) What is the meaning of the term *rpm*?
   Revs per minute (4)
   (ULEAC)

Question 2 and student answer

In Fig. 6.34 you are shown part of the control system for the tailplane of a model aircraft.

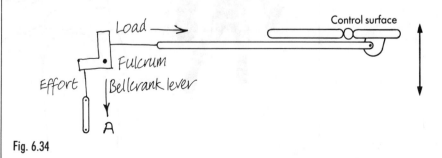

Fig. 6.34

a) Complete the diagram by adding a suitable linkage to move the control surface of the tailplane up and down as rod *A* is moved.

b) Indicate, on the linkage you have drawn, the position of the Fulcrum, Effort and Load.

(6)

(ULEAC)

Question 3 and student answer

Complete the table by selecting from the list of options below.

Fishing reel   Cam   G-Cramp   Chain and Sprocket   Corkscrew
Peg and Slot   Hand Drill   Pulley System

USE	MECHANISM
FISHING REEL	Ratchet and pawl
Bicycle drive system	*CHAIN + SPROCKET*
G CRAMP	Square thread
Valve system on a car engine	*CAM*

(4)

Question 4 and student answer

In Fig. 6.35 you are shown a photograph and diagram of a toy figure. As the lever *A* is pushed down, the figure's arm *B* is raised. When lever *A* is released arm *B* falls.

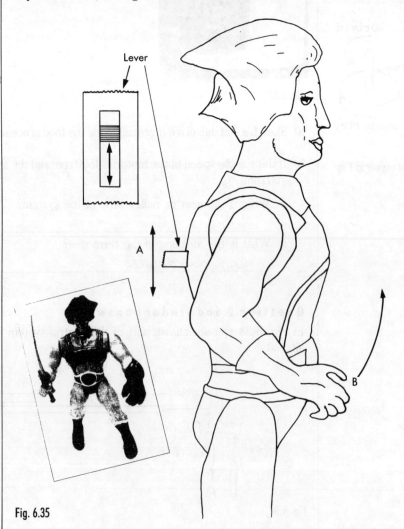

Fig. 6.35

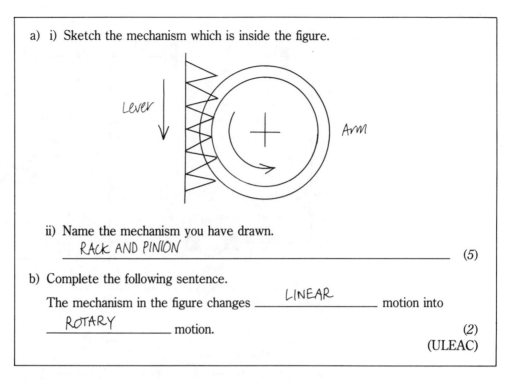

a) i) Sketch the mechanism which is inside the figure.

ii) Name the mechanism you have drawn.
RACK AND PINION

(5)

b) Complete the following sentence.
The mechanism in the figure changes ___LINEAR___ motion into ___ROTARY___ motion.

(2)
(ULEAC)

Fig. 6.36 Student answer to Question 4 a) i)

Remember, using and applying a *mechanical knowledge* is:

■ Easier if you use a 'Black box' or systems approach to the problem.

■ Easier if you practise your knowledge by modelling mechanisms with a kit system.

■ Not to be taken for granted. Because mechanisms are all around it does not mean that we know about or understand them.

As we saw earlier, the application and understanding of *electrical and electronic knowledge* to solving problems is helped by the use of a systems approach. However, before this can be fully used you need to have an idea that an electric current is a flow of charge normally carried by electrons. You will also need an understanding of the differences between parallel and series circuits.

PARALLEL AND SERIES CIRCUITS

Fig. 6.37 shows some examples of parallel and series circuits.

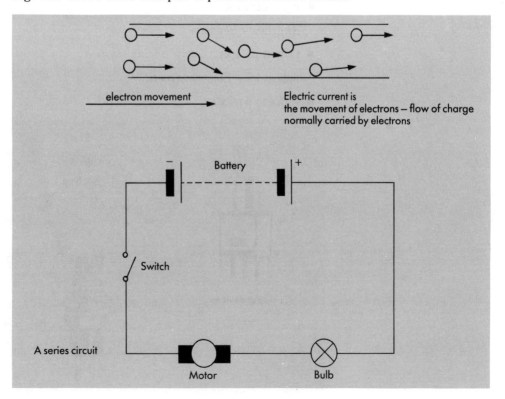

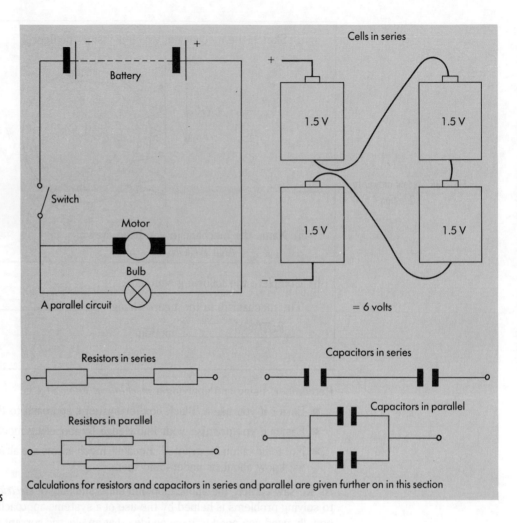

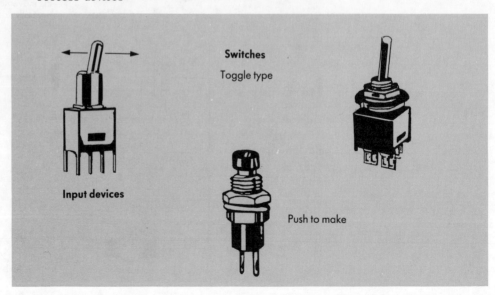

Calculations for resistors and capacitors in series and parallel are given further on in this section

Fig. 6.37 Parallel and series circuits

COMPONENTS

Important components.

You will also need to be able to recognise a range of *components*, together with their circuit symbols, and to identify their uses. In Fig. 6.38 you are shown those components which you need to be most familiar with. They have been grouped as

- Input devices.

  Switches – Sensors.

- Output devices.

  Indicators – Electromagnetic.

- Process devices

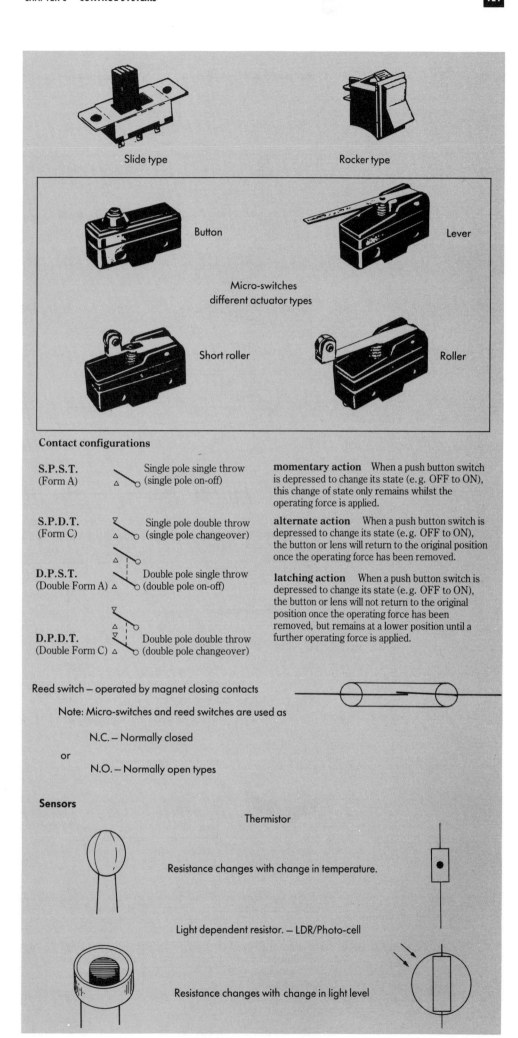

Slide type

Rocker type

Button

Lever

Micro-switches
different actuator types

Short roller

Roller

Contact configurations

S.P.S.T. | Single pole single throw
(Form A) | (single pole on-off)

S.P.D.T. | Single pole double throw
(Form C) | (single pole changeover)

D.P.S.T. | Double pole single throw
(Double Form A) | (double pole on-off)

D.P.D.T. | Double pole double throw
(Double Form C) | (double pole changeover)

momentary action When a push button switch is depressed to change its state (e.g. OFF to ON), this change of state only remains whilst the operating force is applied.

alternate action When a push button switch is depressed to change its state (e.g. OFF to ON), the button or lens will return to the original position once the operating force has been removed.

latching action When a push button switch is depressed to change its state (e.g. OFF to ON), the button or lens will not return to the original position once the operating force has been removed, but remains at a lower position until a further operating force is applied.

Reed switch – operated by magnet closing contacts

Note: Micro-switches and reed switches are used as

N.C. – Normally closed

or

N.O. – Normally open types

Sensors

Thermistor

Resistance changes with change in temperature.

Light dependent resistor. – LDR/Photo-cell

Resistance changes with change in light level

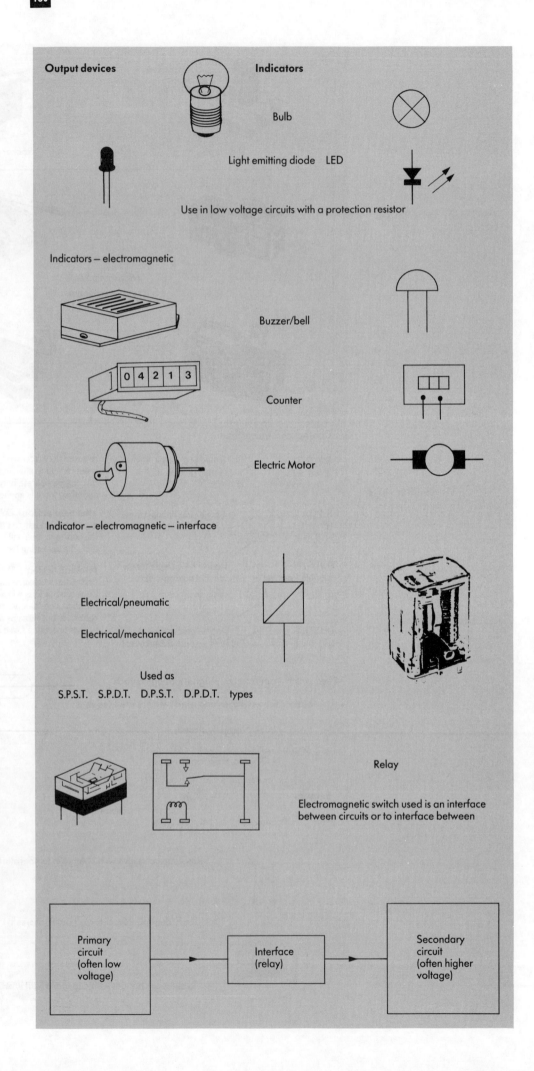

Output devices

Indicators

Bulb

Light emitting diode   LED

Use in low voltage circuits with a protection resistor

Indicators – electromagnetic

Buzzer/bell

Counter

Electric Motor

Indicator – electromagnetic – interface

Electrical/pneumatic

Electrical/mechanical

Used as

S.P.S.T.   S.P.D.T.   D.P.S.T.   D.P.D.T.   types

Relay

Electromagnetic switch used is an interface
between circuits or to interface between

Primary
circuit
(often low
voltage)

Interface
(relay)

Secondary
circuit
(often higher
voltage)

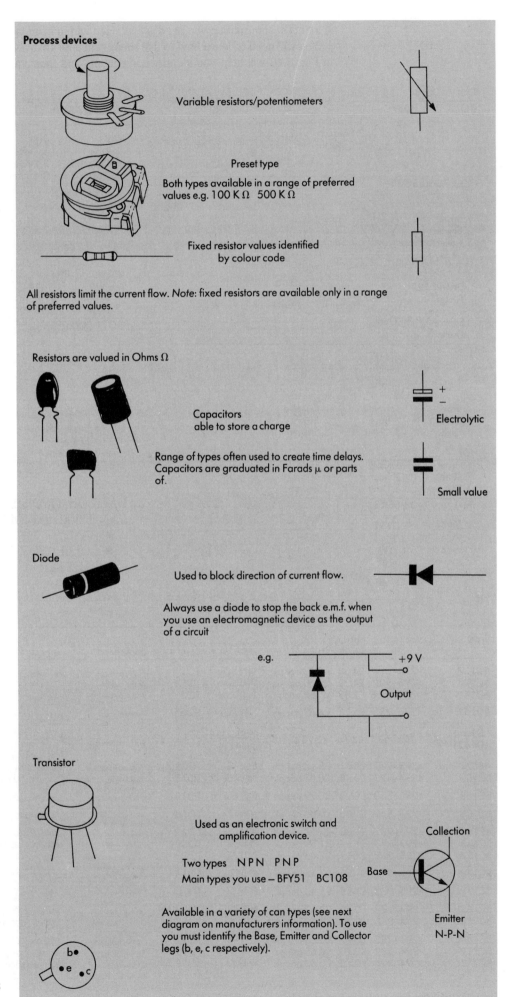

Process devices

Variable resistors/potentiometers

Preset type
Both types available in a range of preferred
values e.g. 100 K Ω   500 K Ω

Fixed resistor values identified
by colour code

All resistors limit the current flow. *Note*: fixed resistors are available only in a range
of preferred values.

Resistors are valued in Ohms Ω

Capacitors
able to store a charge

Electrolytic

Range of types often used to create time delays.
Capacitors are graduated in Farads μ or parts
of.

Small value

Diode

Used to block direction of current flow.

Always use a diode to stop the back e.m.f. when
you use an electromagnetic device as the output
of a circuit

e.g.   +9 V

Output

Transistor

Used as an electronic switch and
amplification device.

Two types   N P N   P N P
Main types you use – BFY51   BC108

Collection

Base

Available in a variety of can types (see next
diagram on manufacturers information). To use
you must identify the Base, Emitter and Collector
legs (b, e, c respectively).

Emitter
N-P-N

Fig. 6.38 Input, output and process
devices

A lot of the information you need is contained within manufacturers' *catalogues* (Fig. 6.39). You will need to learn how to use them, and data such as the *resistor colour* code shown in Fig. 6.40 will help you identify components and their values.

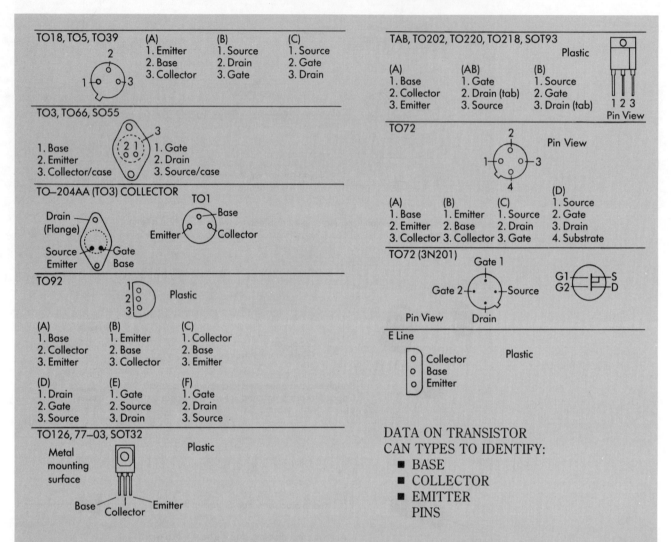

Type	stock no.	price 1–24	25+	material	case	application	P_T	I_C	V_{CED}	V_{CBO}	h_{FE}	f_T(typ)
AC127	*294–621	£4.00	£3.60 per pk	NPN Ge	TO1	Audio output	340mW	500mA	12V	32V	50	2.5MHz
AC128	*293–909	£4.00	£3.60 per pk	PNP Ge	TO1	Audio output	700mW	–1A	–16V	–32V	60–175	1.5MHz
AD149	294–249	£2.03	£1.83 each	PNP Ge	TO3	Audio output	22.5W at 50°C	–3.5A	–50V	–50V	30–100	0.5MHz
AD161 ■	*294–233	£5.13	£4.62 per pk	NPN Ge	SO55	Audio output	4W at 72°C	3A	20V	32V	80–320	3MHz
AD161 ⎫ Pair AD162 ⎭	293–577	£3.64	£3.28 pair	NPN Ge ⎱ PNP Ge ⎰ SO55		Audio matched pair	⎧4W at 72°C ⎨ ⎩6W at 63°C	3A –3A	20V –20V	32V –32V	50–300 50–300	3MHz 1.5MHz
AF127	*293–937	£5.71	£5.14 per pk	PNP Ge	TO72(A)	I.F.Applications	60mW	–10mA	–20V	–20V	150 ◆	75MHz
BC107	*394–527	£0.98	£0.83 per pk	NPN Si	TO18	Audio driver stages (complement BC177)	360mW	00mA	5V	0V	10–450	50MHz
BC108	*293–533	£0.93	£0.79 per pk	NPN Si	TO18	General purpose (complement BC178)	360mW	100mA	20V	30V	110–800	250MHz
BC109	*293–549	£1.05	£0.89 per pk	NPN Si	TO18	Low noise audio (complement BC179)	360mW	100mA	20V	30V	200–800	250MHz
BC142	*293–987	£1.80	£1.51 per pk	NPN Si	TO39	Audio driver	800mW	60V	80V		20(min)	80MHz
BC143	*293–993	£1.87	£1.59 per pk	PNP Si	TO39	Audio driver	800mW	–800mA	–60V	–60V	25(min)	160MHz
BC177	*295–911	£1.58	£1.43 per pk	PNP Si	TO18	Audio driver stages (complement BC107)	300mW	–100mA	–45V	–50V	125–500	200MHz
BC178	*295–927	£1.58	£1.43 per pk	PNP Si	TO18	General purpose (complement BC108)	300mW	–100mA	–25V	–30V	125–500	200MHz
BC179	*295–933	£1.58	£1.43 per pk	PNP Si	TO18	Low noise audio (complement BC109)	300mW	–100mA	–20V	–25V	240–500	200MHz
BC182L	*294–277	£0.70	£0.63 per pk	NPN Si	TO92(A)	General purpose	300Mw	200mA	50V	60V	100–480	150MHz
BC183L	*294–968	£0.60	£0.54 per pk	NPN Si	TO92(A)	General purpose (complement BC213L)	300mW	200mA	30V	45V	100–850	280MHz
BC184L	*294–283	£0.72	£0.65 per pk	NPN Si	TO92(A)	General purpose	300mW	200mA	30V	45V	250(min)	150MHz
BC212L	*294–299	£0.72	£0.65 per pk	PNP Si	TO92(A)	General purpose	300Mw	–200mA	–50V	–60V	60–300	200MHz
BC213L	*294–974	£0.70	£0.63 per pk	PNP Si	TO92(A)	General purpose (complement BC183L)	300mW	–200mA	–30V	–45V	80–400	350MHz

Fig. 6.39 Useful data from catalogues (reproduced by kind permission of RS Components Ltd)

No one is able to hold all of the component detail in their heads. Using reference tables and catalogues is an important part of applying your electrical and electronic knowledge.

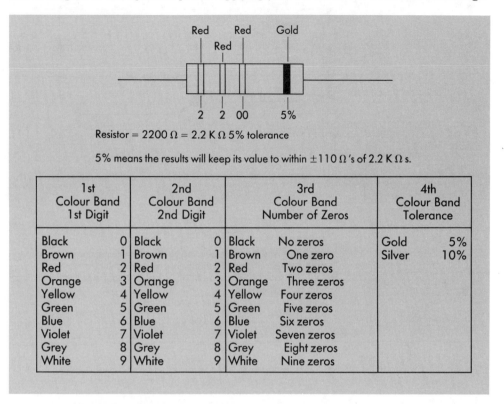

1st Colour Band 1st Digit		2nd Colour Band 2nd Digit		3rd Colour Band Number of Zeros		4th Colour Band Tolerance	
Black	0	Black	0	Black	No zeros	Gold	5%
Brown	1	Brown	1	Brown	One zero	Silver	10%
Red	2	Red	2	Red	Two zeros		
Orange	3	Orange	3	Orange	Three zeros		
Yellow	4	Yellow	4	Yellow	Four zeros		
Green	5	Green	5	Green	Five zeros		
Blue	6	Blue	6	Blue	Six zeros		
Violet	7	Violet	7	Violet	Seven zeros		
Grey	8	Grey	8	Grey	Eight zeros		
White	9	White	9	White	Nine zeros		

Fig. 6.40 Resistor colour code

Fig. 6.41 looks at how, by using a systems approach, you can use a small group of circuits to solve many problems.

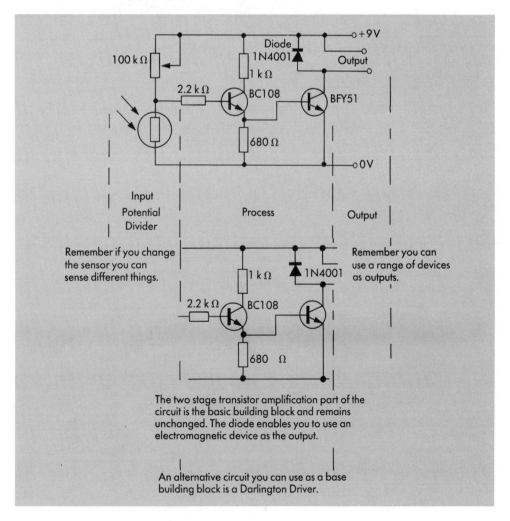

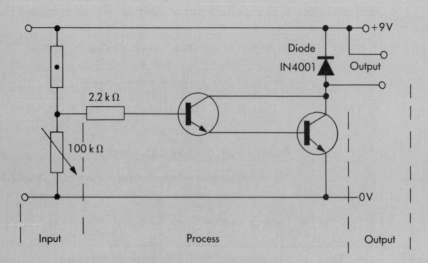

Another basic building block is a multivibrator circuit. This will enable you to flash lights or other output devices on or off. When one light is on the other is off.

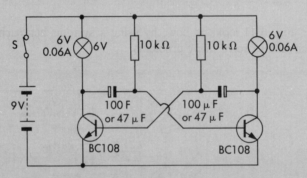

This multivibrator function can also be produced by using a 555 Timer I.C.

If you alter the values of the capacitors or resistors you will change the rate at which the lights flash. Alternatively, you could use a variable resistor in the circuit, as shown below.

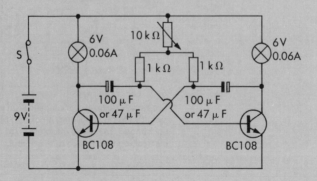

The final building block you need is a time delay circuit. In the time delay circuit shown a Darlington Driver has been used as the Process block, you could also use the two stage transistors amplification circuit we looked at earlier.

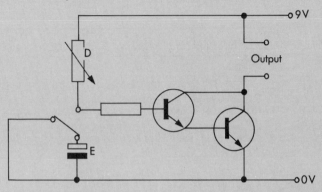

Now you have some basic building blocks you can begin to design solutions to problems.

For example. You are asked to design a circuit which will operate the authomatic watering system of a greenhouse when the soil becomes too dry. The owner of the greenhouse also requires a flashing light to warn when the watering system is operating.

Start by producing a block diagram for the circuit.

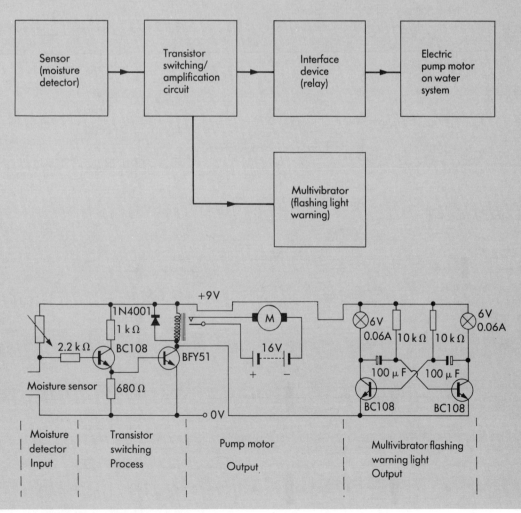

Fig. 6.41 Using a small group of circuits to solve many problems

EQUATIONS AND CALCULATIONS

The following (Fig. 6.42) are examples of the electrical/electronic equations and calculations you need to be familiar with.

▶ **Resistors in series**

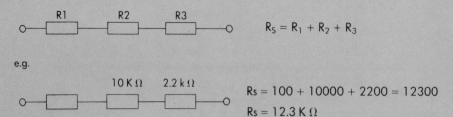

$$R_S = R_1 + R_2 + R_3$$

e.g.

$$Rs = 100 + 10000 + 2200 = 12300$$
$$Rs = 12.3\,K\,\Omega$$

▶ **Resistors in parallel**

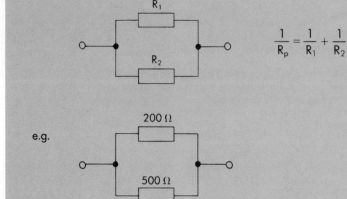

$$\frac{1}{R_p} = \frac{1}{R_1} + \frac{1}{R_2}$$

▶ **Resistors in series and parallel**

e.g.

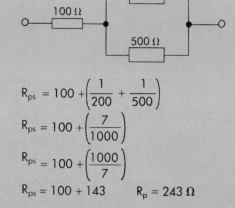

$$\frac{1}{R_p} = \frac{1}{200} + \frac{1}{500}$$

$$\frac{1}{R_p} = \frac{5+2}{1000} \qquad \frac{7}{1000}$$

$$R_p = \frac{1000}{7} \qquad Rp = 143\,\Omega$$

e.g.

$$R_{ps} = 100 + \left(\frac{1}{200} + \frac{1}{500}\right)$$

$$R_{ps} = 100 + \left(\frac{7}{1000}\right)$$

$$R_{ps} = 100 + \left(\frac{1000}{7}\right)$$

$$R_{ps} = 100 + 143 \qquad R_p = 243\,\Omega$$

▶ **Capacitors in parallel**

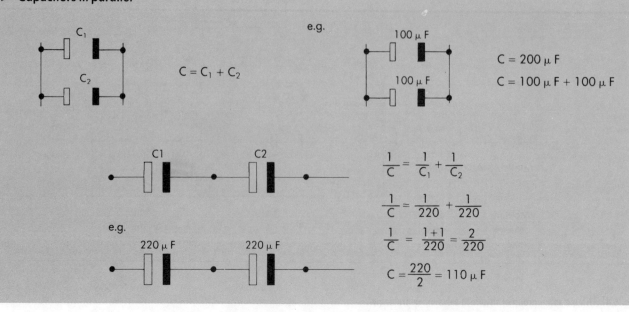

$$C = C_1 + C_2$$

e.g.

$$C = 200\,\mu F$$
$$C = 100\,\mu F + 100\,\mu F$$

$$\frac{1}{C} = \frac{1}{C_1} + \frac{1}{C_2}$$

$$\frac{1}{C} = \frac{1}{220} + \frac{1}{220}$$

$$\frac{1}{C} = \frac{1+1}{220} = \frac{2}{220}$$

$$C = \frac{220}{2} = 110\,\mu F$$

► **Ohm's Law**

voltage = current × resistance or V = I × R

try to remember

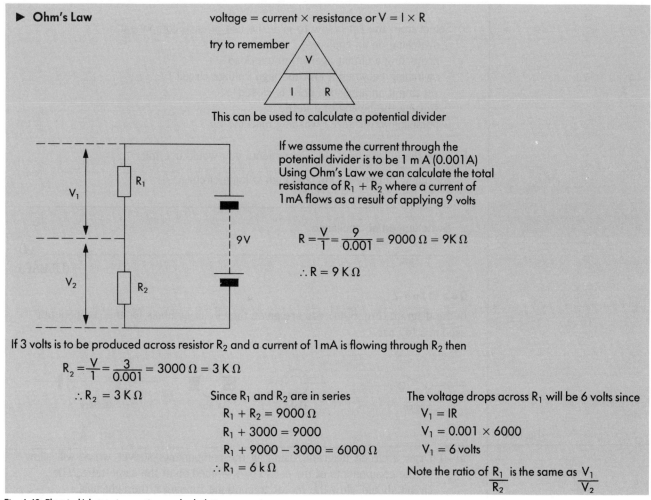

This can be used to calculate a potential divider

If we assume the current through the potential divider is to be 1 m A (0.001A) Using Ohm's Law we can calculate the total resistance of $R_1 + R_2$ where a current of 1mA flows as a result of applying 9 volts

$$R = \frac{V}{I} = \frac{9}{0.001} = 9000 \, \Omega = 9 K \, \Omega$$

$$\therefore R = 9 K \Omega$$

If 3 volts is to be produced across resistor R_2 and a current of 1mA is flowing through R_2 then

$$R_2 = \frac{V}{I} = \frac{3}{0.001} = 3000 \, \Omega = 3 K \, \Omega$$

$$\therefore R_2 = 3 K \Omega$$

Since R_1 and R_2 are in series

$$R_1 + R_2 = 9000 \, \Omega$$
$$R_1 + 3000 = 9000$$
$$R_1 + 9000 - 3000 = 6000 \, \Omega$$
$$\therefore R_1 = 6 \, k \, \Omega$$

The voltage drops across R_1 will be 6 volts since

$$V_1 = IR$$
$$V_1 = 0.001 \times 6000$$
$$V_1 = 6 \text{ volts}$$

Note the ratio of $\frac{R_1}{R_2}$ is the same as $\frac{V_1}{V_2}$

Fig. 6.42 Electrical/electronic equations and calculations

S A M P L E   Q U E S T I O N S

QUESTIONS INVOLVING ELECTRICAL/ELECTRONIC KNOWLEDGE

The following are example questions from the written examination which are testing your electrical/electronic knowledge. There are further examples in Chapter 4.

Question 1

In the diagrams Fig. 6.43, you are shown a range of components often used in the control circuits of kitchen appliances.   (6)

Use

_____

_____

_____

Fig. 6.43

a) Select from the list below to give the use of each component.
   switching on an appliance
   protecting a circuit against an overload
   switching between a low and high voltage circuit
   sensing if an appliance door is closed
   sensing the boiling of a kettle
   pumping water into a washing machine

b) Give the full name of the components you would use for:

   Switching between a low and high voltage circuit.

   _____

   Switching on an appliance.

   _____ *(4)*

(ULEAC)

Question 2

In the diagram (Fig. 6.44) you are given the circuit symbols for the components used in a toy car.

| Switch | Light | Motor | Battery |

Fig. 6.44

a) i) Draw a circuit diagram, using all the components above, which will allow all the components of the car to be switched on at the same time. The circuit should allow the motor to continue running if the light fails.

ii) Complete the following sentence.

   The motor and light in the circuit are connected in _____ *(5)*

b) i) Complete Fig. 6.45 showing how you would connect four of the 1.5 V cells shown, to produce a total of 6 V as the energy source for the toy car.

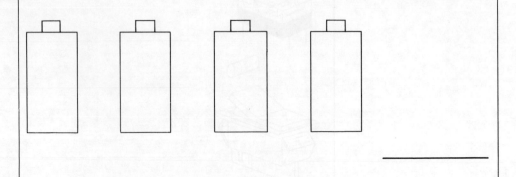

Fig. 6.45

ii) Complete the following sentence.

The four 1.5 V cells must be connected in _____ (3)

(ULEAC)

Question 3

In Fig. 6.46 you are shown part of a circuit which will be used for an automatic greenhouse shading system.

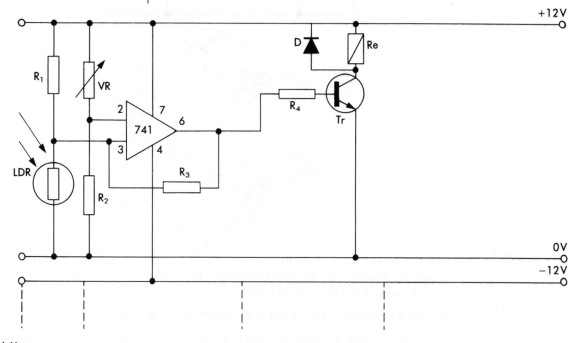

Fig. 6.46

a) i) Complete the diagram of the P.C.B. in Fig. 6.47, indicating the position of each component shown in the circuit diagram. (6)

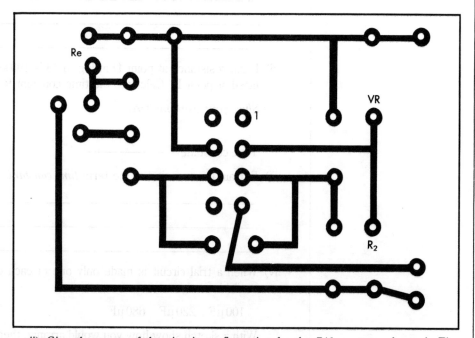

Fig. 6.47

ii) Give the name of the circuit configuration for the 741 op.amp. shown in Fig. 6.46.

_____ (1)

Question 4

In Fig. 6.48 you are shown the circuit diagram and pictorial view of a variable kitchen timer.

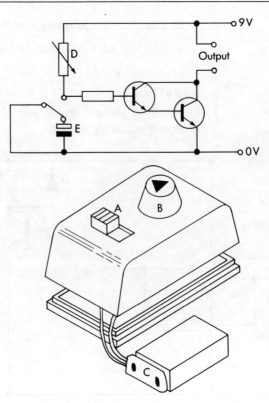

Fig. 6.48

a) Clearly indicate on the circuit diagram which parts are attached to the items marked **A, B** and **C** on the pictorial view.　　　　　　　　　　(6)

b) The manufacturer wishes to extend the range of the timer.

　　i) Explain how the circuit shown in Fig. 6.48 could be modified to do this.

　　　_____

　　　_____

　　　_____

　　　_____ (4)

　　ii) If the resistance at point **D** in Fig. 6.48 is 100 kΩ and a 1000 μF capacitor is fitted at point **E**. Calculate the time constant for the capacitor.

　　　Show your working here.

　　　Time constant = ——————　　　　　　　　　　　　(4)

　iii) Explain the meaning of the term *time constant*.

　　　_____

　　　_____

　　　_____ (2)

　　iv) When a trial circuit is made only one of each of the following capacitors is available:

　　　　100 μF　　220 μF　　680 μF

　　　With a sketch show how you would arrange them to make a total capacitance of 1000 μF.

Remember. You will:

- find it easier to solve problems with a systems approach.
- need to be able to identify components and their circuit symbols.
- have to use data charts and manufacturers' catalogues for information.

A FINAL STATEMENT

- Use a systems approach to solving problems.
- Practise using your mechanical, electrical and electronic knowledge.

This is a very important aspect of all of your work in a CDT: Technology course. However, too often it is forgotten or looked at as an afterthought in your revision. Whilst most of the Examining Groups will test your knowledge in this area through the Common Core paper, it should be a consideration in all of your work.

You should be able to discuss and describe:

- the relationship between technology, the individual and society in terms of economic, cultural, social, ecological and industrial effects.
- some of the beneficial effects of technology on society.
- some of the potentially harmful effects of technology on society.
- the advantages and disadvantages of a technological change from the viewpoints of those affected.

> **Don't neglect the impact of technology on society.**

If you are to be able to do this successfully you will need to build your knowledge over the period of your course.

- Read articles on the effects of technology in the national press/local press – make notes from them.
- Read magazines which have suitable articles, e.g. *New Scientist*.
- Listen to radio and watch appropriate TV programmes.
  All of these, together with your lessons, will help to build an overall awareness of technology in society for you.

Normally, the questions you are asked are on current, topical issues or based on topics set ahead of the examination by your Examining Group.

S A M P L E   Q U E S T I O N S

QUESTIONS INVOLVING TECHNOLOGY AND SOCIETY

The following are example questions which are testing your awareness of technology in society.

Question 1

This question is based on the common core topic, acid rain, as specified in the syllabus. You may need to read the following passage more than once before answering.

As long ago as 1872, the term acid rain was used by Robert Angus Smith, a British chemist, in a book he wrote. It was not until 1926, however, that the Inspector of Freshwater Fisheries in Norway noted that the sudden death of newly hatched salmon in Norwegian waters seemed to be linked to water acidity. Fig. 6.49 shows the production of acid rain.

Damage from acid rain used to be only in areas close to the source of pollution. With the building of much taller chimneys to reduce local pollution, the problem was merely moved farther away, often to a country foreign to the source of the pollution. The Tyneside area of the United Kingdom is possibly the main source of acid rain pollution in Sweden, but the movement of pollutants is a two way process. The 'produced' and 'deposited' figures for sulphur pollution in some European countries are given in the following table.

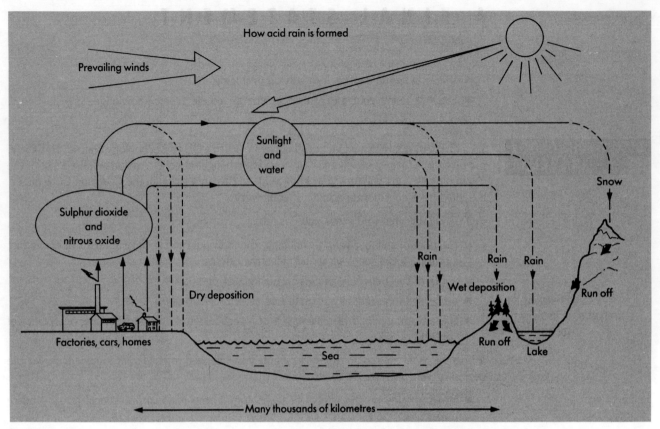

Fig. 6.49

SULPHUR POLLUTION TABLE

Country	Tonnes of sulphur produced (× 1000)	Tonnes of sulphur deposited (× 1000)
Belgium	404	161
France	1800	1212
Germany	1815	1158
Iceland	6	74
Italy	2200	1132
Poland	2150	1330
Sweden	275	472
United Kingdom	2560	847

Attempts are now being made to neutralize acidified lakes, but the process was costing Sweden 1.2 million pounds per year by the end of the 1970s. Sweden now expects to spend large sums of money on this problem every year, as it will be some time before the emission of acidifying substances is significantly reduced.

a) State the year in which the term acid rain was first used.

_____ (1)

b) Name the country which produces the largest amount of sulphur pollution.

_____ (1)

c) Briefly explain why the introduction of taller chimneys led to the "exportation" of pollution.

_____

_____

_____

_____ *(1)*

d) Briefly explain how snow falling on a mountain can affect the acidity of a lake in the valley.

_____

_____

_____ *(1)*

e) Rain is naturally acidic to a small degree, without the addition of pollutants. Name the acid which is present in 'unpolluted' rain.

_____ *(1)*

f) Name **two** acids which are additionally present in acid rain.

1 _____ *(1)*

2 _____ *(1)*

g) Give **two** reasons to explain why Iceland has the lowest figures in the table.

1 _____ *(1)*

2 _____ *(1)*

h) Describe **one** simple method by which acidity of lakes or arable land can be reduced.

_____

_____ *(1)*

i) Suggest **two** methods by which the causes of acid raid could be reduced.

1 _____

_____ *(1)*

2 _____

_____ *(1)*

j) The effects of acid rain on life in lakes are quite far reaching, and not always obvious at first. Write a brief account of how and why fish are affected by an increase in the acidity of their environment,.

_____

_____

_____ *(3)*

(MEG)

Question 2

Attempt **either** part a) **or** part b).

a) 'The use of technology in farming and food preparation has allowed us to adopt very different working and eating habits, in recent years. Perhaps we have welcomed the convenience and freedom created by the technology without considering the consequences.'

Discuss this statement using the recent national debate on food safety to provide at least **three** examples for your answer.

OR

b) 'Technology can be a help or handicap to a society.'

Discuss this statement using the current debate over the use of unleaded petrol to provide at least **three** examples for your answer.

_____

_____

_____

_____

(*Total 10 marks*)
(ULEAC)

A FINAL STATEMENT

Remember to do well you need to be interested in your work.

Remember work hard and to the best of your ability.

Remember CDT: Technology has many parts to the course, few people do well in all of them.

Accept the advice and guidance of your teacher.
Enjoy your course.
GOOD LUCK.

APPENDIX: MATERIALS CHECK LIST

More detailed classifications are available in other parts of this book, especially pages 89–102. Here we present a quick check-list for some important properties of materials and the ways in which they can be used.

TIMBERS

	NAME	APPEARANCE	WORKING PROPERTY	USE
HARDWOODS	English Beech	Pale-brown to white, even texture grain	Turns well on the lathe Can be steam bent	Furniture School desks
	Ramin	Almost white, fine grain	Easy to work Only suitable for indoors	Furniture Dowelling Handles
	Teak	Golden brown with dark markings	Hard to work by hand Machines well	Outdoor furniture
	Obeche	Pale-straw yellow Silky sheen Interlocking grain Reddish-brown heart	Easy to work Very light to handle	Most indoor work General use Furniture
SOFTWOODS	European Redwood	Pale yellow	Quality varies Can be worked well with hand tools	Paper Outdoor work when treated with preservative
	Western Red Cedar	Pale pinkish brown, distinctive growth rings	Easy to work with sharp tools Finishes well	Garden furniture Greenhouses

Fig. A.1 Six important timbers

FERROUS METALS

NAME	ALLOY OF:	PROPERTIES	USES
Mild steel	Carbon 0.1–0.3% Iron 99.9–99.7%	Tough. High tensile strength. Can be case hardened. Rusts very easily	Most common metal used in school workshops
Carbon steel	Carbon 0.6–1.4% Iron 99.4–98.6%	Tough. Can be hardened and tempered	Cutting tools and punches
Stainless steel	Iron, nickel and chromium	Tough. Resistant to rust and stains	Cutlery, medical instruments
Cast iron	Carbon 2–6% Iron 98–94%	Strong but brittle. Compressive strength very high. Has a natural lubricant	Castings, manhole covers, engines
Wrought iron	Almost 100% iron	Fibrous, tough, ductile, resistant to rusting	Ornamental gates and railings. Not in much use today

Fig. A.2 Five important ferrous metals

NON-FERROUS METALS

NAME	COLOUR	ALLOY OF:	PROPERTIES	USES
Aluminium	Light grey	Aluminium 95% Copper 4% Manganese 1%	Ductile, soft, malleable, machines well. Very light	Window frames, aircraft, kitchen ware
Copper	Reddish brown	Not an alloy	Ductile, can be beaten into shape, Conducts electricity and heat	Electrical wiring, tubing, pans, kettles, bowls
Brass	Yellow	Mixture of copper and zinc 65%–35% most common ratio	Hard. Casts and machines well Surface tarnishes Conducts electricity	Parts for electrical fittings, ornaments
Silver	Whitish grey	Mainly silver but alloyed with copper to give sterling silver	Ductile, malleable, solders, resists corrosion	Jewellery, solder, ornaments
Lead	Bluish grey	Not an alloy	Soft, heavy, ductile, loses its shape under pressure	Solders, pipes, batteries, roofing

Fig. A.3 Five important non-ferrous metals

PLASTICS

Polyvinyl chloride PVC	Polythene	Expanded polystyrene	Polystyrene	Nylon	Acrylic	Polyurethane	Epoxy resin	Polyester resin	Melamine formaldehyde	MATERIAL	PROPERTY
										THERMO PLASTICS → cols 1–6; THERMOSET PLASTICS → cols 7–10	
											Heavy weight
✓	✓		✓	✓	✓	✓	✓	✓	✓		Medium weight
		✓									Very light weight
							✓	✓	✓		Hard
✓	✓					✓					Medium
✓	✓	✓	✓	✓	✓						Soft
✓	✓		✓	✓	✓	✓	✓	✓	✓		Moisture resistant
											Attractive natural finish
					✓	✓					Colourful
✓	✓				✓				✓		Hard wearing
✓	✓		✓	✓	✓	✓	✓	✓	✓		Stable
✓				✓	✓						Insulate electricity
		✓									Insulate temperature
	✓	✓									Inflammable
✓							✓	✓	✓		Non-inflammable
											Conduct electricity
											Excellent for conducting electricity
✓	✓		✓	✓	✓						Easily bend if heated
											Easily bend cold
											Will bend with treatment
✓	✓					✓	✓	✓	✓		Rigid
✓	✓				✓						Flexible

Fig. A.4 Some properties of plastics

JOINING MATERIALS

SITUATION	MATERIAL							
	Wood/wood	Wood/metal	Acrylic/acrylic	PVC rigid/PVC rigid	PVC flex/PVC flex	Fabric/fabric	Paper card/paper card	Balsa
Contact (allows adjustment by sliding the joint)	PVA	Epoxy	Tensol Nos 12 and 70				Copydex, PVA	Cement
Contact made directly (adjustment cannot be made)	Epoxy contact	Epoxy contact		Contact cement			Copydex contact	
Construction of models	PVA	Epoxy	Tensol No. 12	PVC Contact cement Glue Gun PVC	Contact cement	PVA Plastisol	Copydex	Cement
Hand pressure	Epoxy rapid	Epoxy rapid	Tensol No. 12 Super Glue	Contact cement		PVA	Copydex	Cement
Jewellery	PVA	Epoxy	Tensol No. 12	Contact cement				
Long setting time (more than 5 mins)	PVA	Synthetic	Tensol No. 70 1hr Tensol No. 12 3 hrs	Contact cement		PVA	PVA	
Quick setting time (less than 5 mins)	Epoxy rapid 3–5 mins Glue gun 20–60 sec	Epoxy rapid	Super Glue	Glue gun, PVC Grey 80–90 secs		Glue Gun, black	Copydex contact	Cement
Strength	Synthetic	Epoxy	Tensol No. 12 Super Glue	Contact cement		Plastisol		
Sustained pressure, vice clamp, etc.	PVA	Synthetic						
Temporary	Masking tape	Masking tape	Masking tape	Masking tape	Masking tape	Masking tape	Masking tape, Blue Tack	Masking tape, Blue Tack
Units storage	PVA	Epoxy	Tensol No. 12	Contact cement				
Wet	Synthetic	Epoxy, synthetic	Tensol No. 70	Contact cement		Plastisol		Cement

Fig. A.5 Bonding materials together

SITUATION	METALS						
	Mild steel/ mild steel	Aluminium/ aluminium	Copper/ copper	Gilding/ gilding	Cast iron/cast iron	Tin plate/tin plate	Brass/brass
General	Brazing spelter 870°C	Ali brazing	Soft solder Silver solder, Sil fos	Silver solder	Cast iron gas arc	Soft solder B	Silver solder
Low melting range	Soft solder A 183–185°C	Silver solder No. 2 Soft solder A	Easy Flo No. 2 608°– 617°C			Soft solder A	
High melting range	Soft solder V 183°–276°C Brazing spelter		Soft solder V Silver solder C4 740°– 780°C				Silver solder
Strength important	Oxy- acetylene welding						
Tack together	Arc welding		Silver solder		Arc welding		
Electrical circuits			Multi core resin flux				Multi core
Sweating	Soft solder A Tinmans 183°–185°C		Soft Solder A Tinmans 183°–185°C			Soft solder A Tinmans 183°–185°C	

Fig. A.6 Selecting a soldering or welding process

FINISHES

Improve performance	Improve appearance	Protection	Polyvinyl chloride PVC	Polythene	Polystyrene (expanded)	Polystyrene (opaque)	Nylon	Acrylic	Polyester Resin	Plastic Laminate	Gilding metal	Brass	Copper	Aluminium	Wrought iron	Cast iron	Stainless steel	Carbon steel	Mild steel	Boards (general use medium quality)	Veneer boards (with attractive grain)	Hardboard	Western red cedar	European redwood	Obeche	Teak	Ramin	English beech	FINISH
	✓	✓																			✓			✓	✓		✓	✓	Bees wax
	✓																											✓	Carnauba wax
✓																								✓				✓	Paraffin wax
✓	✓	✓																			✓			✓	✓		✓	✓	Silicon wax
	✓	✓																								✓			Teak oil
	✓																							✓			✓		Raw linseed oil
		✓																	✓										Mineral oil
	✓	✓																			✓			✓	✓		✓		Varnish
	✓																						✓	✓	✓			✓	Stain
	✓	✓																			✓			✓	✓		✓	✓	Lacquer 'single pack'
✓	✓	✓																		✓			✓	✓		✓	✓	Lacquer 'two pack'
	✓											✓	✓								✓			✓	✓		✓	✓	Lacquer cellulose
	✓	✓																			✓				✓		✓		French polish
	✓																						✓						Creosote
	✓	✓																					✓						Wood preservative
	✓	✓											✓						✓										Enamelling
✓	✓	✓												✓															Anodising
✓		✓																✓											Plastics coating
	✓										✓		✓	✓															Planishing
	✓															✓		✓	✓										Wire brush
	✓												✓						✓										Tempering oxides
	✓	✓														✓			✓										Red heat oxides
	✓	✓												✓					✓										Hammer finish paint
	✓											✓				✓			✓										Crackle finish paint
	✓				✓															✓		✓							Emulsion paint
	✓	✓											✓			✓			✓	✓		✓		✓					Polyurethane coloured
	✓					✓							✓																Cellulose coloured
	✓								✓																				Colouring pigment
✓								✓																					Anti-static cleaner

Fig. A.7 Types of finish for various materials

INDEX